The Grand Tour: Qurānic Descriptions of Paradise

Shaykh Azhar Nasser

Dedication

"The first person to enter Paradise is Fātima."
-The Holy Prophet

I dedicate this book to Fātima bint Muhammad, who according to traditions will be the first person to enter Paradise. I pray that this humble contribution to the blessed religion of her father will earn me the honor of her intercession.

Foreword

In the name of the Almighty
May Allāh bless the Prophet Muhammad & his purified
progeny.

I had the opportunity to glance through the draft of *The
Grand Tour: Qur'ānic Descriptions of Paradise* by Shaykh
Azhar Nasser. The issues related to the life in the hereafter is
of great interest to the believers and has been frequently
mentioned in the Qur'ān.

The themes of the subject have been divided by Shaykh
Nasser in a way that appeals to the reader. While discussing
the verses of the Qur'ān, Shaykh Nasser has referred to the
credible sources of the Shi'a literature and has refrained from
imposing personal opinions over the Qur'ān. And this indeed
is commendable in the era where writers try to straitjacket the
Qur'ān with the society's current trends.

May the Almighty accept this endeavour and grant the author
more tawfīqāt.

Sayyid Muhammad Rizvi
14 March 2018

Acknowledgments

I thank God first and foremost, for His infinite grace in enabling me to complete this endeavor. Without His unceasing aid, I am powerless, incapable, and helpless. It is solely through His providence that any goodness can be conceived and achieved.

Secondly, I would like to thank my late grandfather, Dr. Kadhum Saied, for instilling the love of the Holy Qurān in my heart when I was a child. I pray that one day we are reunited in Paradise in the company of the Holy Prophet and his immaculate family.

I also wish to extend my gratitude to my loving wife, Laya, for her encouragement and passionate support. She has been an outstanding life partner and any book I write, half of the credit goes to her.

I would also like to thank my two beautiful children, Alī and Zainab, for being my small taste of Paradise in this earthly life. I implore God to protect you both and guide you to His pleasure.

Finally, I would like to thank Aaliya Sheriff for designing the cover of this book and Behi Behbahani for her efforts in editing the manuscript.

Table of Contents

Dedication 3

Foreword 5

Acknowledgments 7

Table of Contents 9

Introduction 11

Chapter One: The Existence of Paradise **15**

Chapter Two: The Path to Paradise **25**

Faith and Righteous Deeds 27

Piety 30

Virtuousness 31

Resisting Lowly Desires 33

The Foremost in Faith 35

Patience 37

Sincerity 39

Repentance 40

Attention to Prayer 42

Compassion for Creation 46

Association and Denouncement 49

Truthfulness 51

Charity 52

Purification of the Soul 55

Chapter Three: Material Blessings of Paradise **59**

Gardens and Rivers 62

Ample Shade 67

The Palaces 68

The Furniture 71

The Food 76

The Drinks 81

The Best Drink 86

The Dishware 87

The Garments 90

The Jewelry 91
The Spouses and Maidens............................ 93
The Servants... 97
The Hosts 98
Incomprehensible Delights 99

Chapter Four: The Spiritual Blessings of Paradise 103
Distinct Reverence 106
Ambiance of Peace 109
Neither Grief nor Fear................................ 111
Intimate Friends and Devoted Companions.............. 113
Pleasant Social Interactions 116
Inner Peace and Outer Joy 118
God's Pleasure 120
Inner Witnessing and Loving Attention.................... 123
Whatever Their Souls Desire 126
Unfathomable Bounties 128
Eternal Bliss 129

Chapter Five: The Gates, Vastness and Stations of Paradise.. 131
The Gates 133
The Vastness 142
The Stations 145

Index.. 153

Introduction

The existence of a life after death is a central theme in the Islamic tradition, and one of the core tenets of faith. With approximately 1400 verses in the Holy Qurān revolving around the concept of eternal life, there is no denying that death is merely a gateway to a world that is tremendously vaster than the human mind can begin to comprehend. If death is the first station of the hereafter, then Paradise and Hellfire are its final abodes. The Holy Qurān is replete with descriptive accounts of both Paradise and Hellfire. However, in this holy book, God invariably delves into more vivid and nuanced portrayals of the indulgences and delights of Paradise than the graphic horrors of the Hellfire. From this, one could reasonably construe that God is more eager to reward than to chastise, and more keen on blessing than banishing.

Paradise is the focal point of Divine favors and the locus of God's countless blessings. It contains pleasures and enjoyments that even the height of imagination cannot reach. The Holy Qurān entices the human being with the prospect of incomprehensible reward when it says,

فَلا تَعلَمُ نَفسٌ ما أُخفِيَ لَهُم مِن قُرَّةِ أَعيُنٍ جَزاءً بِما كانوا يَعمَلونَ

"No one knows what has been kept hidden for them of comfort as a reward for what they used to do."[1]

---

[1] Qurān 32:17

11

Thus, for us to gain even a rudimentary appreciation of this coveted dwelling place, we will refer to the Qurānic descriptions of Paradise and the reports of the Ahlul Bayt[2] (a.s.). These verses and narrations contain breathtaking accounts of the residents of Paradise, its lush gardens, flowing rivers, gushing springs, succulent foods, refreshing drinks, opulent garments, exquisitely beautiful maidens, youthful servants, splendid palaces and lavish furnishings. In addition to these material enjoyments, the Qurān asserts that Paradise also offers spiritual rewards in the form of angelic salutations, the companionship of God's righteous servants, God's loving attention, pleasant social interactions, inner peace and the exhilaration of Divine proximity. With that said, the book before you will explore the following themes:

1. The existence of Paradise
2. The path to Paradise
3. The material blessings of Paradise
4. The spiritual blessings of Paradise
5. The gates, vastness, and stations of Paradise

I sincerely hope that this book incentivizes and motivates believers to tirelessly strive towards moral excellence and seize any opportunity to do good. Often times, we are ambitious about our worldly activities but settle for mediocrity in our spiritual undertakings. I pray that this humble work provides the impetus for Muslims to cultivate high spiritual ambitions and seek the loftiest stations of Paradise.

The Day of Judgment is also called the 'Day of Remorse' for

---

[2] The Ahlul Bayt (a.s.) are a reference to the Holy Prophet (s.a.), Fatima his daughter, Ali ibn Abi Talib (a.s.) his cousin and son in law, Hassan and Hussain (a.s.) his grandsons and the nine imams from the progeny of Hussain (a.s.).

it is a day of deep regret for both believers and disbelievers alike.

The disbelievers will drown in sorrow, for squandering the gift of life, while the believers will feel the sting of disappointment, for not attaining even higher stations of Paradise. Imam Zaynul Abideen[3] (a.s.) is reported to have said,

مَعاشِرَ شيعَتِنا! أمَّا الجِنَّةُ فَلَن تَفُوتَكُم سَرِيعاً كانَ أو بَطِيناً ولكِنْ تَنافَسُوا في الدَّرَجاتِ.

"O our followers! As for Paradise, it will not escape you sooner or later, but do compete with each other to attain stations therein." [4]

---

[3] Imam Zaynul Abidīn (a.s.) is the fourth holy imam and the great grandson of the Holy Prophet (s.a.). He lived between 38 AH and 95 AH.
[4] Bihar al-Anwār, v. 74, p. 308, no. 61

Chapter One: The Existence of Paradise

All Muslims unanimously affirm that the promise of God is true and that reward awaits the pious while an agonizing chastisement looms over the heads of the wicked. God's perfection dictates that He always fulfills His promise. The breaking of a promise connotes inability, ignorance or regret, all of which are beneath the Glory and Perfection of the Divine Essence. The Holy Qurān asserts in many verses that God never breaks His promises. One such example is,

$$ إِنَّ اللّٰهَ لاَ يُخْلِفُ الْمِيعَادَ $$

"Indeed God does not break His promise." [5]

Therefore, all of humankind can anticipate a generous recompense if they tread the path of godliness, and fear the dreadful punishment if they choose a life of iniquity and rebelliousness. The question that naturally arises when discussing Paradise is whether it presently exists or will be created in the future.

---

[5]   Qurān 3:9

17

We can infer from the Holy Qurān and the traditions of the Ahlul Bayt (a.s.), that not only is Paradise real but that it already exists. For instance, the Holy Qurān in a few verses states that Paradise has already been prepared for the good doers. The following verses establish this fact,

وَسَارِعوا إِلَى مَغْفِرَةٍ مِن رَبِّكُم وَجَنَّةٍ عَرضُهَا السَّماواتُ وَالأَرضُ أُعِدَّت لِلمُتَّقِينَ

"*And hasten towards your Lord's forgiveness and a Paradise as vast as the heavens and the earth, prepared for the pious.*"
[6]

سَابِقُوا إِلَى مَغْفِرَةٍ مِّن رَّبِّكُمْ وَجَنَّةٍ عَرْضُهَا كَعَرْضِ السَّمَاء وَالْأَرْضِ أُعِدَّتْ لِلَّذِينَ آمَنُوا بِاللَّهِ وَرُسُلِهِ

"*Take the lead towards forgiveness from your Lord and a Paradise as vast as the heavens and the earth, prepared for those who have faith in God and His messengers.*"[7]

The word أُعِدَّت is a past tense verb which means "prepared", and some Quranic exegetists contend that its usage indicates that Paradise exists at the present moment. This is the belief held by the overwhelming majority of Twelver Shī'i theologians, and some notable Sunni scholars. Al-Qurtubi, the prominent Mālikī scholar of hadīth has stated,

"It is the view of the majority of Muslim scholars that Paradise has been created and presently exists. The narrations regarding the Prophet's ascension explicitly confirm this as well as many other narrations in the two sahīh's [Bukhārī and Muslim]."[8]

---

[6] Qurān 3:133
[7] Qurān 57:21
[8] Tafsīr al-Qurtubi, v. 2, p. 1447

Another verse that confirms the present existence of Paradise is the verse relating to the Holy Prophet's ascension. The Holy Qurān says,

$$\text{وَلَقَد رَآهُ نَزلَةً أُخرِ عِندَ سِدرَةِ المُنتَهىٰ عِندَها جَنَّةُ المَأوى}$$

"Certainly he saw him, yet another time, by the Lote Tree of the Ultimate Boundary, near which is the Garden of Refuge."
9

According to some commentators of the Holy Qurān, this verse refers to one of the two instances in which the Prophet is said to have seen the Archangel Gabriel in his true form. The Holy Prophet is said to have seen Gabriel's true form only twice, once at Mount Hira, where he received the first revelation, and a second time during the Ascension. "The Lote Tree of the Ultimate Boundary" is an elusive expression that has invoked a wide range of interpretations, however, for the sake of brevity and simplicity, we can infer that the Holy Prophet saw the angel Gabriel in his true form at this mysterious tree in the "Garden of Refuge", which is one of the names of Paradise in the Qurān.

There are also numerous narrations that support the notion of an already-existing Paradise. We will explore a small sample of narrations as further evidence to substantiate this position. One of the companions of Imam Alī ibn Mūsa al-Ridhā (a.s.), once asked the Imam whether Paradise and Hellfire were already created, to which the Imam replied,

$$\text{وإنَّ رسول الله صلَّى الله عليه وآله قد دخل الجنَّة ورأى النار لمّا عرج به إلى}$$
$$\text{السماء}$$

---

9 Qurān 53:13-15

19

"Verily, the Messenger of God entered Paradise and saw the Hellfire when he was made to ascend to the heavens." [10]

The narrator then proceeded to inform the Imam that some people believe that Paradise and Hellfire will be created after the destruction of the temporal world. The Imam retorted,

ما أولئك منّا ولا نحن منهم ، من أنكر خلق الجنّة والنار فقد كذّب النبيّ صلّى الله عليه وآله وكذّبنا

"They are not from us nor are we from them. He who rejects the creation of Paradise and Hellfire belies the Prophet and belies us." [11]

There are also other narrations in Sunni and Shīa hadīth literature relating to the conception of Lady Fātima (a.s.) that confirm the current existence of Paradise. One hadīth reports:

لما عرج بي الى السما اخذ بيدي جبرائيل فادخلني الجنة فناولني من رطبها فاكلته فتحوّل ذلك نطفة في صلبي فلما هبطت الى الارض واقعت خديجة فحملت بفاطمة ففاطمة حورا انسية فكلما اشتقت الى رائحة الجنة شممت رائحة ابنتي فاطمة

The Holy Prophet states, "When I was made to ascend towards heaven, Gabriel took hold of my hand and escorted me into Paradise and offered me its fruits, so I ate. Then that [fruit] transformed into a life-seed in my loins. When I descended to the earth, I approached Khadija and she became pregnant with Fātima. Thus, Fātima is a heavenly human being. Whenever I yearn for the fragrance of Paradise, I smell the fragrance of my daughter, Fātima." [12]

---

[10] Bihār al-Anwār, v. 8, p. 119
[11] Bihār al-Anwār, v. 8, p.119
[12] al-Mustadrak, v. 6, p. 156

This narration establishes the current existence of Paradise by explicitly highlighting that the Holy Prophet was escorted into Paradise by the Archangel Gabriel. Furthermore, Gabriel offers the Prophet its fruits from which the life-seed of Lady Fātima is generated. If Paradise is to be created after the collapse of the universe as we know it, the abovementioned narration would be rendered utterly meaningless.

The Holy Qurān also speaks about the consumption of the provisions of Paradise by one of the holiest women in the Islamic tradition, Mary, the mother of Jesus Christ (a.s.). Mary, the daughter of Imran, spent most of her time worshipping in her private prayer chamber at the local temple. Her guardian, Prophet Zackariah (a.s), regularly visited her in her sanctuary and noticed something miraculous about this young lady. The Holy Qurān says,

كُلَّما دَخَلَ عَلَيها زَكَرِيّا المِحرابَ وَجَدَ عِندَها رِزقًا ۖ قالَ يا مَريَمُ أَنّى لَكِ هٰذا ۖ قالَت
هُوَ مِن عِندِ اللَّهِ ۖ إِنَّ اللَّهَ يَرزُقُ مَن يَشاءُ بِغَيرِ حِسابٍ

"Whenever Zackariah visited her in the sanctuary, he would find provisions with her. He said, 'O Mary, from where does this come for you?' She said, 'It comes from Allah. Allah provides whomever He wishes without any reckoning." [13]

Some commentators say that Mary would have had the fruits of summer in the winter and of the winter in summer. As such, there is a tradition from the Holy Prophet that asserts that the provisions originated from Paradise.

In one hadīth, the Prophet praises his daughter after witnessing the descent of heavenly food upon her,

---

[13] Qurān 3:37

21

الحمد لله الذي جعلك شبيهة بسيدة نسا بني اسرائيل

"Praise be to God who has likened you [Fātima] to Mary, the mistress of the Children of Israel."[14]

There are also narrations that suggest that Paradise is in a state of perpetual construction and expansion. It is the deeds and actions of the human being that supply Paradise with the raw materials for its ongoing creation. Similar to the manner in which rainfall and sunlight foster the growth of plant life in a lush tropical forest, so too do our good deeds give life to our personal paradisal experience. Such a view would only be plausible if Paradise was currently in existence. It is reported that the sixth Holy Imam (a.s.), Imam al-Sadiq once said,

من قال سبحان الله غرس الله له بها شجرة في الجنة , ومن قال الحمد لله غرس الله له بها شجرة في الجنة , ومن قال لا اله الا الله غرس الله له بها شجرة في الجنة , ومن قال الله اكبر غرس له بها شجرة في الجنة فقام له رجل من قريش كان بين الحاضرين وقال له : اذن فشجرنا في الجنة اكثر , فقال له النبي : نعم ولكن اياكم ان ترسلوا عليها نيرانا فتحرقوها

"He who says, 'Glory be to God', God will plant a tree in Paradise for him. And he who says, 'All praise belongs to God', God will plant a tree in Paradise for him. And he who says, 'God is great', God will plant a tree in Paradise for him. Then a man from Quraysh stood among the attendees and said, "In that case, our trees in Paradise are many". To which the Holy Prophet (s.a.) replied, "Yes, but be weary not to send fire upon them and burn them [with your sins]." [15]

---

[14] Tafsīr al-Ayyāshī in his commentary on Sūrah 3:37
[15] Bihār al-Anwār, v. 8, p. 186

22

In another hadīth, the Holy Prophet (s.a.) shares a fascinating discovery about the continual genesis of Paradise during his illustrious ascension:

لما اسري بي الى السما دخلت الجنة فرايت فيها ملائكه يبنون لبنة من ذهب ولبنة من فضّة , وربماامسكوا , فقلت لهم : مالكم ربما بنيتم وربما امسكتم؟ فـقالوا حتى تجيئنا النفقة سبحـان الله والـحمد لله ولا اله الا الله والله اكبر , فاذا قال بنينا , واذا امسك امسكنا

> "When I was made to ascend to Heaven, I entered Paradise and saw angels building [using] gold and silver bricks. Sometimes they would stop. So I asked them, 'Why is it that sometimes you build and other times you halt?' They replied, 'We wait for raw materials [of God's remembrance in the form of] 'Glory be to God', 'All praise belongs to God', 'There is no god but God' and 'God is great'. If one recites, we build, and if he stops, we also stop'."[16]

Even this small sample of Qurānic verses and the handful of narrations mentioned above serve as sufficient evidence to confirm the current existence of Paradise. Not only does it exist but it is actively being constructed by God's angels who await these raw materials of righteousness and God consciousness. In conclusion, one can reference a powerful excerpt from the renowned Allāmah Bāqir al-Majlisī's[17] voluminous "Oceans of Lights" where after presenting the verses and hadīth that confirm the creation of Paradise before the destruction of this worldly life says,

---

[16] Bihār al-Anwār, v. 8, p. 186
[17] Allāmah Bāqir al-Majlisī was the most influential of all Shia scholars of the Safavid era. He lived from 1037 AH to 1111 AH.

"Know that the belief in Paradise and Hellfire as presented by the verses [of Qurān] and the narrations [of Ahlul Bayt] without [metaphorical] interpretation is an established tenet of faith. The one who rejects it or interprets it [in contrast to its apparent meaning] as the philosophers have done, has defected from religion. As for the present creation [of Paradise and Hellfire], it is the view of the majority of Muslims aside from a minority of Mu'tazilites...It seems that no one from the Twelver Shī'i [scholars] supports [the Mu'tazilite view] except what has been attributed to Sayyid al-Razī."[18]

---

[18] Bihār al-Anwār, v. 8, p. 205. Sayyid Abul-Hasan Muhammad ibn Al-Husayn Al-Musawi is known as Sayyid al-Razī for short. He was a Shia scholar and poet who lived from 359 AH to 406 AH. He is best known for his compilation of Nahj al-Balāgha.

Chapter Two: The Path to Paradise

The Holy Qurān speaks at length, not only about the delights and pleasures of Paradise, but also the deeds that enable man to reach Paradise and revel in its lofty stations. From an Islamic perspective, salvation and eternal prosperity require self-struggle: a tenacious and rigorous commitment to self-refinement. It necessitates the acquisition of noble traits, and the purging of morally vile characteristics. In this chapter, we will explore some of the Qurānic verses that discuss the various paths that lead the human being to the gardens of bliss.

Faith and Righteous Deeds

وَالَّذِينَ آمَنوا وَعَمِلُوا الصّالِحاتِ أُولئِكَ أَصحابُ الجَنَّةِ هُم فيها خالِدونَ

"And those who have faith and do righteous deeds, —they shall be the inhabitants of Paradise; they shall remain in it [forever]." [19]

Faith provides the ideological foundation for human existence. It also presents the criterion through which to distinguish moral good from moral evil, right from wrong, and righteousness from wickedness. It is through the mechanisms of faith that we bind ourselves to a system of belief that impacts the personal, social, economic, religious and spiritual dimensions of our lives. Faith offers a moral framework and an ethical standard for our behavior in this world. However, faith alone does not suffice.

True faith is manifested through word coupled with action. Historically, many religious traditions have stressed that faith alone is the path to salvation and redemption. The Qurān consistently highlights the fact that faith and righteous deeds are intertwined and unexclusive of one another. In fact, the Qurān purports that Paradise will not be gained through belief that is void of action, and similarly, it will not be granted on the basis of racial or tribal affiliations. The Holy Qurān informs us that some of the Children of Israel considered themselves to be the chosen ones among God's creation, despite the absence of morality in their conduct. They believed that God would only punish them in the Hellfire for a short while and that they would ultimately be granted Paradise on account of their superficial adherence to faith, irrespective of their deeds. The Qurān quotes them as saying,

وَقَالُوا لَن تَمَسَّنَا النَّارُ إِلَّا أَيَّامًا مَّعْدُودَةً ۚ قُلْ أَتَّخَذْتُمْ عِندَ اللَّهِ عَهْدًا فَلَن يُخْلِفَ اللَّهُ عَهْدَهُ ۖ أَمْ تَقُولُونَ عَلَى اللَّهِ مَا لَا تَعْلَمُونَ

---

[19] Qurān 2:82

28

"And they say, 'The Fire shall not touch us except for a number of days.' Say, 'Have you taken a promise from God? If so, God shall never break His promise. Or do you ascribe to God what you do not know?'" [20]

One can think of the relationship between faith and righteous deeds as analogous to the relationship of a tree to its fruits. True faith underlies the genesis of all good deeds in the same way that a healthy tree yields wholesome fruit. Good, purified deeds are of such great significance that salvation is dependent on good actions. And in return, good actions always emanate from sincere intentions. When Imam al-Sādiq (a.s.) was asked to explain the reality of faith, he said,

الإيمان أن يطاع الله فلا يعصى

"[True] Faith is to obey God and not disobey Him." [21]

The Imam in this hadīth, binds faith to obedience. Obedience is related to action and conduct, and thus, faith and action are inextricable. When studying the Holy Qurān, one finds that faith and righteous deeds are often paired together. Whenever God mentions the quality of faith, he couples it with the performance of good deeds. Imam Alī, in a famous tradition warned Muslims of the danger of allowing themselves to become satisfied with the notion of religiosity based solely on belief and faith alone. The Imam (a.s.) once said,

لا تكن ممّن يرجو الآخرة بغير العمل

---

[20] Qurān 2:80
[21] Usūl al-Kāfī, v. 2, p. 33

"Do not be among those who hope for the hereafter without acting…" [22]

Piety

تِلكَ الْجَنَّةُ الَّتِي نُورِثُ مِن عِبادِنا مَن كانَ تَقِيًّا

"That is the Paradise We will give as inheritance to those of Our servants who are God-conscious." [23]

The invitation towards God-consciousness is a recurring theme throughout Qurānic discourse. The word تقوى is an Arabic term that is derived from the word وقاية which literally means 'to protect' or 'to safeguard'. In the Qurān, its usage conveys a mind-set of hypersensitivity to Divine commandments whereby the individual cautiously discharges his duties and actively avoids sins. Put simply, God-consciousness is essentially fulfilling religious obligations and abstaining from acts of disobedience. Islamic ethicists have delineated the notion of God-consciousness by asserting that it is a state of hyper-vigilance against falling into sin out of negligence. It is the idea that a believer is always on guard and is perpetually alert to any action that would earn the displeasure of the Almighty. It is the state of preparedness in anticipation of a situation where one might be pressured into committing sin, that serves as a precursor to avoiding such environments altogether. In its higher forms, God-consciousness is the fear of not taking the most paramount path towards God's grace.

---

[22] Nahj al-Balāgha, Saying 150
[23] Qurān 19:63

There is a plethora of narrations which highlight the true reality of taqwa, but for the sake of succinctness we will draw on an excerpt from Imam Alī (a.s.)'s famous sermon where he masterfully describes the people of taqwa in saying,

يَعمَلُ الأعمالَ الصّالِحَةَ و هُو عَلَى وَجَلٍ، يُمسِي وَهَمُّهُ الشُّكرُ، ويُصبِحُ وَهَمُّهُ الذِّكرُ، يَبِيتُ حَذِراً، ويُصبِحُ فَرِحاً؛ حَذِراً لِما حُذِّرَ مِن الغَفلَةِ، وفَرِحاً بِما أصابَ مِنَ الفَضلِ والرَّحمَةِ؛ إنِ استَصعَبَت عَلَيه نَفسُهُ فِيمَا تَكرَهُ لَم يُعطِها سُؤلَها فِيمَا تُحِبُّ؛ قُرَّةُ عَينِه فِيمَا لا يَزولُ، وزَهادَتُهُ فِيمَا لا يَبقَى، يَمزُجُ الحِلمَ بِالعِلم والقَولَ بِالعَمَلِ؛ تَراهُ قَرِيباً أمَلُهُ، قَلِيلاً زَلَلُ، خاشِعاً قَلبُهُ، قانِعَةً نَفسُهُ، مَنزُوراً أكلُهُ، سَهلاً أمرُهُ، حَرِيزاً دِينُهُ، مَيِّتَةً شَهوَتُهُ، مَكظُوماً غَيظُهُ، الخَيرُ مِنهُ مَأمُولٌ، والشَّرُّ مِنهُ مَأمُونٌ

"He performs virtuous deeds but still feels afraid. In the evening, he is anxious to offer thanks [to God]. In the morning, his anxiety is to remember [Allah]. He passes the night in fear and rises in the morning in joy - fear, lest night is passed in forgetfulness, and joy over the favor and mercy received by Him. If his self refuses to endure a thing which it does not like, he does not grant its request towards what it likes. The coolness of his eye lies in what is to last forever, while from the things [of this world] that will not last he keeps aloof. He transfuses knowledge with forbearance, and speech with action. You will see his hopes simple, his shortcomings few, his heart fearing, his spirit contented, his meal small and simple, his religion safe, his desires dead, and his anger suppressed. Good alone is expected from him. Evil from him is not to be feared." [24]

Virtuousness

لَهُم ما يَشاءونَ عِندَ رَبِّهم ۚ ذٰلِكَ جَزاءُ المُحسِنِينَ

---

[24] Nahj al-Balāgha Sermon 193

"They will have whatever they wish near their Lord. That is the reward of the virtuous." [25]

The word إحسان (*ihsān*) has no accurate English translation as it is a word that encompasses a multitude of noble traits. It is a spiritual status whereby an individual has combined servitude to God with complete certainty and conviction. A محسن (*muhsin*) is one who does good and strives for excellence because they feel the profound presence of God and keenly sense His ever-watchful eye.

Some Islamic scholars explain إحسان as being the *inner* dimension of Islam whereas sharīah is often described as the *outer* dimension:

"It should be clear that not every Muslim is a man or woman of faith (mu'min), but that every person of faith is a Muslim. Furthermore, a Muslim who believes in all the principles of Islam may not necessarily be a righteous person (a doer of good), but a truly good and righteous person is both a Muslim and a true person of faith." [26]

رُوِيَ أَنَّ النَّبِيَّ صَلَّى اللهُ عَلَيْهِ وَآلِهِ سُئِلَ عَنِ الإِحْسَانِ، فَقَالَ: أَنْ تَعْبُدَ اللهَ كَأَنَّكَ تَرَاهُ، فَإِنْ لَمْ تَكُنْ تَرَاهُ فَإِنَّهُ يَرَاكَ.

It is reported that the Prophet (s.a.) was asked about *ihsān*, to which he replied, "It is to worship God as if you see Him; for verily even if you do not see Him, indeed He sees you." [27]

---

[25] Qurān 39:34
[26] Islam: Faith and History, p. 54
[27] Nūr al-Thaqalayn, v. 1, p. 553

Resisting Lowly Desires

وَأَمَّا مَنْ خَافَ مَقَامَ رَبِّهِ وَنَهَى النَّفْسَ عَنِ الْهَوَىٰ فَإِنَّ الْجَنَّةَ هِيَ الْمَأْوَىٰ

"But as for him who is fearful to stand before his Lord and forbids the soul from [following] desire, his refuge will indeed be Paradise." [28]

Undoubtedly, there is a deep interconnection between fear of God and resisting lowly desires. This fear eventually evolves into a deep attachment and love of God that conquers the depths of the human soul. Resulting from this, the soul begins to crave spiritual nourishment and consequently abstains from any lowly desires that tarnish it and stunt its growth. Islamic ethicists maintain that the root of all corruption and wickedness that transpires on the face of the earth can be traced back to blind submission to worldly desires. They also assert that the sole remedy is instilling fear of God into the heart. Throughout human history, the most worshipped objects other than God have been lowly desires and worldly passions. It is reported that the Holy Prophet once said,

ما تحت ظل السماء من إله يعبد من دون الله أعظم عند الله من هوىً متبع

"There is no deity under the sky that is more grave with God than desires that are followed." [29]

---

[28] Qurān 79:40-41
[29] Tafsīr Dur al-Manthūr, v. 5, p. 72

The Holy Qurān also declares that, among human beings, are those who follow their desires so blindly that it is as though they have taken them as objects of worship. God, Almighty says,

أَرَأَيتَ مَنِ اتَّخَذَ إِلَهَهُ هَواهُ

"Have you seen him who has taken his desire to be his god?" [30]

It is noteworthy to mention that the Qurān underscores two antithetical qualities to fear of God and resisting lowly desires, as the two main traits that inevitably lead man to the Hellfire: rebellion and attachment to the worldly life. The Qurān highlights these destructive qualities when it says,

فَأَمَّا مَن طَغَىٰ وَآثَرَ الحَياةَ الدُّنيا فَإِنَّ الجَحيمَ هِيَ المَأوىٰ

"As for him who was rebellious and preferred the life of this world, his refuge will indeed be Hell." [31]

Rebellion and attachment to the temporal world are regarded as the source of man's misery, while fear of God and the taming of lowly desires are considered the fountainhead of prosperity and enduring happiness.

In contrast, Islamic mystics have identified seven passions to be the root of all sin. This conclusion is based on the following verse which lists seven desires that serve as the seeds from which all sins sprout. The Holy Qurān states,

زُيِّنَ لِلنَّاسِ حُبُّ الشَّهَواتِ مِنَ النِّساءِ وَالبَنينَ وَالقَناطيرِ المُقَنطَرَةِ مِنَ الذَّهَبِ وَالفِضَّةِ وَالخَيلِ المُسَوَّمَةِ وَالأَنعامِ وَالحَرثِ

---

[30] Qurān 25:43
[31] Qurān 79:37-39

34

"Beautified for people is the love of that which they desire - of women and sons, heaped-up sums of gold and silver, fine branded horses, and cattle and tilled land." [32]

This verse alludes to a common theme connecting all human beings to their ephemeral desires. Elsewhere, the Holy Qurān calls upon man to express gratitude for these worldly blessings, however, in this context the seductive side is brought into focus. A believer is instructed to enjoy the bounties of this earthly life without developing attachments that distract one from the ultimate purpose of life, achieving unlimited happiness and pleasure through nearness to God.

The Foremost in Faith

Historically, the emergence of any new faith has been met with hostility and fierce opposition since new religious movements often challenge the status-quo of their communities. New religious traditions call into question some of the most long standing values and principles upon which many a culture and civilization has been built. With the advent of Islam, the beliefs, ideals and practices of 7th century Arabia were strongly contested. Consequently, those who joined Islam early on, faced a malicious onslaught of verbal and physical abuse. Therefore, the foremost in faith under such severe conditions enjoy unmatched merit for their praiseworthy resilience. They are the spirited minority who swam against the current of the overwhelming majority, placing their wealth, and in some cases, their lives in harm's way.

---

[32] Qurān 3:14

It is through their perseverance and unwavering devotion that the religion permeated through the far reaches of the earth and extended to future generations. The Holy Qurān mentions those foremost in faith, as being the elite among God's servants who enjoy a special distinction in the Hereafter:

وَالسَّابِقُونَ السَّابِقُونَ أُولَٰئِكَ الْمُقَرَّبُونَ فِي جَنَّاتِ النَّعِيمِ

"And the Foremost Ones are the foremost ones: they are the ones brought near [to God], [who will reside] in the gardens of bliss." [33]

The word السَّابِقُونَ derives from the verb سَبَقَ meaning 'to go first', 'to go ahead', 'to outstrip' or 'to win a race'. The commentaries vary in identifying *the foremost*. Many interpretations identify this group as the first to accept Islam, the first members of the religious community or the sincere who are the first in responding to the call of God and spare nothing in seeking His pleasure. Other commentaries suggest *the foremost* are the first ones to come towards the canonical daily prayers, the first to seek repentance, the first to set out in the way of God, or those who are leading in attaining virtue. The Qurān asserts that, it is the foremost who are nearest to God and the ones who will be granted residency in the highest parts of Paradise. Some traditions also suggest that the foremost will not be subject to the reckoning before God on the Day of Judgment, and that they will proceed straight to Paradise. Some narrations mention four individuals as being prime examples of those who belong to this group[34]:

1. Abel (Adam's pious son)
2. The believer among the family of Pharaoh[35]

---

[33] Qurān 56:10-12
[34] Bihār al-Anwār, v. 66, p. 156
[35] This individual is referenced in Surah 40, verse 28 and is identified by narrations to be Ezekiel

3. Habīb al-Najjār (who's tragic martyrdom is alluded to in Surat Yāsīn)
4. Imam Ali ibn Abi Tālib [36]

Patience

وَجَزاهُم بِما صَبَروا جَنَّةً وَحَريرًا

"And He rewarded them for their patience with a garden and [garments of] silk." [37]

Patience is one of the paramount virtues and the holy grail of the spiritual wayfarers. However, it is often misunderstood as a form of 'silent suffering', whereby the bitterness of a misfortune is tolerated without protest or complaint. Rumi, the 13th century Persian poet, accurately captured the essence of patience when he said,

"Patience is not sitting and waiting, it is foreseeing. It is looking at the thorn and seeing the rose, looking at the night and seeing the day. Lovers are patient and know that the moon needs time to become full."

God describes the attitude of the patient ones in the Holy Qurān when He says,

وَلَنَبْلُوَنَّكُم بِشَيءٍ مِنَ الخَوفِ وَالجوعِ وَنَقصٍ مِنَ الأَموالِ وَالأَنفُسِ وَالثَّمَراتِ
وَبَشِّرِ الصّابِرينَ الَّذينَ إِذا أَصابَتهُم مُصيبَةٌ قالوا إِنّا لِلَّهِ وَإِنّا إِلَيهِ راجِعونَ

---

[36] Tafsīr Nūr al-Thaqalayn, v. 5, p. 209
[37] Qurān 76:12

"We will surely test you with a measure of fear and hunger and a loss of wealth, lives, and fruits; and give good news to the patient. Those who, when an affliction visits them, say, 'Indeed we belong to God, and to Him do we indeed return." [38]

It has been decreed by God that the human being will inevitably face various forms of difficulty and affliction in this worldly life. Only through trial and tribulation can the soul develop and ultimately flourish. In the same way, the body must undergo a rigorous workout regimen to facilitate muscle growth, the soul requires hardship to mature and acquire noble traits. In this verse, the mindset of the patient is summarized in recognizing two important realities, *"Indeed, we belong to God"*, which points to God's absolute ownership of all things, and secondly, *"and to Him do we indeed return"*, which signifies the eventual return of all things to Him.

When the human being acknowledges that God is the true owner of all the things he thought he owned, it makes the experience of loss less painful. The patient one sees all his possessions as a generous loan from the Beneficent Lord who honored him with this temporary trust. Thus, when he loses wealth, health, or a loved one, he sees the loss in its true light, a return to its original owner. The idea of all things returning to God serves as a stark reminder of the fleeting nature of pain and suffering. No matter how bitter the calamity, one should know that pain is temporary and one day it will undoubtedly subside.

Islamic ethicists contend that patience should not be limited to dealing with trial and tribulation. In fact, patience is regarded as a multi-dimensional virtue. The Commander of the Faithful,

---

[38] Qurān 2:155-156

Alī ibn Abī Tālib (a.s.) explains that there are three types of patience:

الصَّبْرُ: إِمّا صَبْرٌ عَلَى الْمُصيبَةِ، أو عَلَى الطّاعَةِ، أو عَنِ الْمَعصيَةِ، وهَذا الْقِسمُ الثّالِثُ أعلَى دَرجَةً مِنَ القِسمَينِ الأوّلَينِ

"Patience comes in the form of either persevering in the face of an affliction, or enduring an act of obedience, or restraining oneself against an act of disobedience. And this third type is of a higher caliber than the first than the first two." [39]

Sincerity

إِنّا أَنزَلنا إِلَيكَ الكِتابَ بِالحَقِّ فَاعبُدِ اللَّهَ مُخلِصًا لَهُ الدِّينَ

"Indeed, We have sent down the Book to you with the truth; so worship God, offering Him sincere devotion." [40]

The word إخلاص in the Holy Qurān, as well as hadīth literature, refers to the sincerity of intention whereby the human being directs all efforts in hopes of gaining the pleasure of God. Islamic mystics regard sincerity as the highest station of love and servitude to God. The renowned mystic, Khwājah `Abd Allah al-Ansāri says, "Sincerity means purging action of all impurities".[41]

By employing the term 'impurities', he means the desire to please oneself and other creatures. The sincere are the those

---

[39] Sharhe Nahj al-Balāgha li Ibn Abī al-Hadīd, v. 1, p. 319
[40] Qurān 39:2
[41] Manāzil al-Sāirīn, p. 88

who worship God in such a way that they do not see themselves in service nor do they take notice of the world or its people, thus they and their actions entirely belong to Lord. Their state of worship is the path that God Almighty has chosen for Himself and cleared it from the impurity of polytheism.

Traditions of Ahlul Bayt (a.s.) indicate that on the Day of Judgement, it is the quality of one's deeds that carry more weight than the quantity of deeds. And it is precisely this notion of sincerity of intention that elevates the quality of one's deeds. A few good deeds coupled with sincerity will suffice on the Day of Resurrection as opposed to numerous deeds void of sincerity. The following narration attests to this important concept:

فِيمَا نَاجَى اللهُ تَبَارِكَ وتَعَالَى مُوسَى عَلَيهِ السَّلامُ: يا مُوسَى! ما أُرِيدَ بِهِ وَجْهِي فَكَثِيرٌ قَلِيلُهُ، وما أُرِيدَ بِهِ غَيرِي فقَلِيلٌ كَثِيرُه

"God, Almighty, addressed Prophet Moses in intimate conversation saying, 'O Moses, whatever is done for My sake, a little of it is a lot and whatever is done for the sake of others, a lot of it is little." [42]

Repentance

يا أَيُّهَا الَّذِينَ آمَنوا توبوا إِلَى اللَّهِ تَوبَةً نَصوحًا عَسىٰ رَبُّكُم أَن يُكَفِّرَ عَنكُم سَيِّئَاتِكُم وَيُدخِلَكُم جَنَّاتٍ تَجري مِن تَحتِهَا الأَنهارُ

---

[42] al-Kāfī, v. 8, p. 46

"O you who have faith! Repent to Allah with sincere repentance! Maybe your Lord will absolve you of your misdeeds and admit you into gardens with streams running in them." [43]

Repentance means the return to the soul's initial spirituality after the light of its human nature (*fitrah*) has been covered by the darkness of sins and disobedience. The human soul in its initial state is pure, sinless and has an inherent light. The perpetration of sin causes obscurity within the heart, and the light of the *fitra* is extinguished and converted into darkness. However, before total darkness envelops the heart, if a person awakens from the slumber of negligence and sincerely repents, the soul gradually returns from the darkness to the light of its original nature.

Repentance is not accepted from one who merely declares, "I repent". There are several conditions that must be fulfilled before repentance is accepted by God. These are mentioned below in the following hadīth:

اَلِاسْتِغْفَارُ دَرَجَةُ الْعِلِّيِّينَ وَ هُوَ اسْمٌ وَاقِعٌ عَلَى سِتَّةِ مَعَانٍ أَوَّلُهَا اَلنَّدَمُ عَلَى مَا مَضَى وَ اَلثَّانِي اَلْعَزْمُ عَلَى تَرْكِ الْعَوْدِ إِلَيْهِ أَبَداً وَ اَلثَّالِثُ أَنْ تُؤَدِّيَ إِلَى اَلْمَخْلُوقِينَ حُقُوقَهُمْ حَتَّى تَلْقَى اَللَّهَ عَزَّ وَ جَلَّ أَمْلَسَ لَيْسَ عَلَيْكَ تَبِعَةٌ وَ اَلرَّابِعُ أَنْ تَعْمِدَ إِلَى كُلِّ فَرِيضَةٍ عَلَيْكَ ضَيَّعْتَهَا فَتُؤَدِّيَ حَقَّهَا وَ اَلْخَامِسُ أَنْ تَعْمِدَ إِلَى اَللَّحْمِ اَلَّذِي نَبَتَ عَلَى اَلسُّحْتِ فَتُذِيبَهُ بِالْأَحْزَانِ حَتَّى تُلْصِقَ اَلْجِلْدَ بِالْعَظْمِ وَ يَنْشَأَ بَيْنَهُمَا لَحْمٌ جَدِيدٌ وَ اَلسَّادِسُ أَنْ تُذِيقَ اَلْجِسْمَ أَلَمَ اَلطَّاعَةِ كَمَا أَذَقْتَهُ حَلَاوَةَ اَلْمَعْصِيَةِ فَعِنْدَ ذَلِكَ تَقُولُ أَسْتَغْفِرُ اَللَّهَ

Imam Alī (a.s.) says,

"Verily, seeking forgiveness [from God] is a degree of the 'illiyyun', translated as 'people of high station', and it is a word that means six things

[43] Qurān 66:8

41

The first is remorse over the past, the second is the resolution not to return to it ever, the third is to return to creatures their (formerly usurped) rights so that you meet God Almighty in a state of purity in which no one has any claim against you. The fourth meaning is that you fulfil every duty that you neglected to satisfy your obligation in respect to it, the fifth is that you attend to the flesh of your body that has grown on unlawful nourishment so that it melts away because of grief and mourning and your skin adheres to your bones, after which new flesh grows in its place. Finally, the sixth is that you make your body taste the pain of obedience in the same way as it earlier tasted the pleasure of sins. When you have done these things then say astaghfirullah!"[44]

This noble tradition mentions two prerequisites for repentance: remorse and resolution, two important conditions for its acceptance: returning the rights of creatures and of the Creator, and finally two points for the perfection of repentance: the shedding of flesh that has grown as a result of unlawful consumption and subjecting the body to the pain of obedience as a disciplinary measure.

Attention to Prayer

There is no ritual in the Islamic tradition that occupies a more central role in the life of a Muslim than the five daily prayers.

---

[44] Nahj al-Balāgha saying 417

It is perhaps the only religious ritual that has been mandated to be performed multiple times a day. The Holy Qurān routinely makes mention of the outstanding qualities of the believers, and gives attention to prayer exceptional primacy. Establishing prayer is of such paramount importance to spiritual development that it has been prescribed upon even the most elite of God's servants. God Almighty quotes the great messenger of God, Jesus (a.s.) son of Mary as saying,

$$وَأَوْصَانِي بِالصَّلَاةِ وَالزَّكَاةِ مَا دُمْتُ حَيًّا$$

"...and He has enjoined me to [maintain] the prayer and to [pay] the zakat as long as I live." [45]

Prayer is nourishment for the human soul. In the same way the body cannot survive without food, the soul also demands regular sustenance. Some mystics assert that the heart is analogous to a plant while prayer is like water. The plant will always require water and similarly every spiritual wayfarer will always need prayer.

Failure to perform the obligatory prayer is considered one of the most serious offenses and may ultimately lead one to the punishment of the Hellfire.

The Hellfire in the Islamic tradition is seen by many, as a sort of spiritual hospital with short-term patients, long-term patients, and a few suffering from terminal spiritual diseases. The following verse captures a conversation between some of the inmates of Hell and its angelic keepers:

$$مَا سَلَكَكُم فِي سَقَرَ قَالُوا لَم نَكُ مِنَ الْمُصَلِّينَ$$

---

[45] Qurān 19:31

43

"What drew you into Hell? They will answer, 'We were not among those who prayed'." [46]

The ritual prayer represents a unique invitation from God, extended to man to enjoy a formal audience with Him. It is through the daily prayer that the human being is able to maintain a constant connection with his Lord. Abandoning it, is tantamount to pulling the plug of spiritual life support from a fragile creature. For this reason, as illustrated by the above-mentioned verses, when the angels ask the sinners what drove them to Hell, the first iniquity that is mentioned, is the abandonment of prayer. The willful neglect of the prayer makes the soul vulnerable to heedlessness, which in turn makes it susceptible to a wide range of lethal spiritual maladies.

The Holy Qurān not only instructs Muslims to perform the daily prayers, but also speaks of the manner in which prayers should be offered. God Almighty says,

قَد أَفلَحَ الْمُؤمِنونَ الَّذينَ هُم في صَلاتِهِم خَاشِعونَ

"Certainly, the faithful have attained salvation, those who are humble in their prayers." [47]

The Qurān asserts that the true believers offer their prayers in a state of complete humility. They are fully cognizant of the overwhelming presence of the Creator that they stand before. Many contemporaries of Imam al-Hassan (a.s.) witnessed this type of humbleness when he prepared for his daily prayers. In one narration, an onlooker describes the condition of the Imam as he performed the ablution in preparation for prayer,

---

[46] Qurān 74:42-43
[47] Qurān 23:1-2

كانَ الحَسَنُ عَلَيهِ السَّلامُ إذا تَوَضَّأَ تَغَيَّرَ لَوْنُهُ، وارتَعَدَت مَفاصِلُهُ، فَقِيلَ لَهُ في ذلكَ، فَقالَ: حَقٌّ لِمَن وَقَفَ بَينَ يَدَي ذِي العَرشِ أن يَصفَرَّ لَوْنُهُ وتَرتَعِدَ مَفاصِلُهُ

"When Imam al-Hassan (a.s.) used to perform his ablution, the color of his face would change and his limbs would tremble. When he was asked about this once, he replied, 'It is only befitting for one who stands before the Lord of the Throne that his face should change color and his limbs should tremble'."
[48]

The prayer is the altar of Divine mercy and the faithful are called upon to hasten towards it as seen in the following verse:

وَسارِعوا إلىٰ مَغفِرَةٍ مِن رَبِّكُم وَجَنَّةٍ عَرضُهَا السَّماواتُ وَالأرضُ أُعِدَّت لِلمُتَّقِينَ

"And hasten towards your Lord's forgiveness and a Paradise as vast as the heavens and the earth, prepared for the pious."
[49]

Many have understood "your Lord's forgiveness" as a reference to the canonical prayers because prayer is an act of spiritual cleansing, likened in some traditions to bathing five times a day. Imam al-Sādiq (a.s.) in one narration explains,

لَو كانَ على بابِ أَحَدِكم نَهرٌ فَاغتَسَلَ مِنهُ كُلَّ يَومٍ خَمسَ مَرّاتٍ هَل كانَ يَبقَى على جَسَدِهِ مِنَ الدَّرَنِ شَيءٌ ؟ إنَّما مَثَلُ الصَّلاةِ مَثَلُ النَّهرِ الّذي يُنقِي، كُلَّما صَلَّى صَلاةً كانَ كَفّارَةً لِذُنوبِهِ

"If there was to be a river outside one's house into which he bathed five times a day, would there remain any dirt on his body? Similarly, the prayer is the river which purifies [one's soul] – every time one performs a prayer, it acts as atonement

[48] Bihār al-Anwār, v. 80, p. 346
[49] Qurān 3:133

45

for one's sins." [50]

In addition to the presence of heart and the awareness of the profound presence of God during the prayer, the Holy Qurān also exhorts the believers to be punctual in performing their prayers. The Holy Prophet (s.a.) regularly stressed the importance of praying on time through his words and actions. Imam Alī (a.s.), in describing the priority the Holy Prophet (s.a.) gave to his prayers once said,

كَانَ رَسُولُ اللهِ صَلَّى اللهُ عَلَيهِ وَآلِهِ لا يُؤْثِرُ عَلَى الصَّلاةِ عَشَاءً ولا غَيرَهُ، وكانَ
إذا دَخَلَ وَقْتُها كَأنَّهُ لا يَعرِفُ أهلاً ولا حَمِيماً.

"The Prophet never put anything before his prayer, neither his dinner nor anything else. When the time for prayer would set in, it was as if he knew neither family nor close friend." [51]

Compassion for Creation

God Almighty has introduced Himself to creation, as the exceedingly Merciful and Compassionate. When God declared that man would serve as His vicegerent on earth, the expectation for this unique being was to reflect the sublime attributes of God. God's creatures are His metaphorical family, and the most beloved to God, are those who treat this family with tender love and care. Everything in creation falls under one of three categories of:

1. Inanimate creatures (stones, stars, water, etc.)
2. Irrational creatures (plants and animals)

---

[50] Bīhar al-Anwār, v. 82, p. 326
[51] Tanbīh al-Khawātir, v. 2, p. 87

3. Rational creatures (humans)

With respect to inanimate creatures, human beings have a moral duty to act as stewards of the environment and pass on the copious resources of the earth to subsequent generations. Furthermore, the Holy Qurān asserts that even the inanimate creatures possess a level of awareness, and they glorify God:

تُسَبِّحُ لَهُ السَّمَاوَاتُ السَّبْعُ وَالأَرْضُ وَمَن فِيهِنَّ وَإِن مِّن شَيْءٍ إِلاَّ يُسَبِّحُ بِحَمْدَهِ
وَلَـكِن لاَّ تَفْقَهُونَ تَسْبِيحَهُمْ

"The seven Heavens glorify Him, and the Earth [too], and whoever is in them. There is not a thing but celebrates His praise, but you do not understand their glorification." [52]

The knowledge that even inanimate beings praise and glorify God, compels one to treat them with sacredness, for in many cases they are more conscious of their Creator than human beings.

Islam also encourages its adherents to be kind to plants and animals. Many traditions strongly discourage the cutting down of fruit trees. Imam al-Sādiq (a.s.) condemned the destruction of fruit-yielding trees when he said,

لا تَقْطَعُوا الثِّمَارَ فَيَبْعَثُ اللهُ عَلَيكُمُ العَذَابَ صَبّا

"Do not cut down fruit trees for God will pour down punishment upon you." [53]

Not only did the Holy Prophet (s.a.) and the Ahlul Bayt (a.s.) criticize those who destroyed vegetative life, rather they actively encouraged people to plant trees.

---

[52] Qurān 17:44
[53] al-Kāfī, v. 5, p 264

47

The Holy Prophet (s.a.) once said,

ما مِن مُسلِمٍ يَزرَعُ زَرعاً أو يَغرِسُ غَرساً فَيَأكُلُ مِنهُ طَيرٌ أو إِنسانٌ أو بَهيمَةٌ إِلّا كانَت لَهُ بِهِ صَدَقَةٌ

"Every single Muslim that cultivates or plants anything of which humans, animals or birds may eat from is counted as charity towards them on his behalf." [54]

During the lifetime of the Prophet (s.a.), the pre-Islamic Arabs had no concept of animal rights and were disgracefully abusive to them. The Holy Prophet gradually awoke their sense of compassion towards animals by asserting that in many cases, animals remember God more than humans. In one hadīth, the Prophet (s.a.) is reported to have rebuked those who mistreated their horses, camels, and donkeys:

رَكِبُوا هَذِهِ الدَّوابَّ سالِمَةً واتَّدِعُوها سالِمَةً، ولا تَتَّخِذُوها كَراسِيَّ لأحادِيثِكُم في الطُّرُقِ والأسواقِ، فَرُبَّ مَركُوبَةٍ خَيرٌ مِن راكِبِها وأكثَرُ ذِكراً لِلَّهِ تَبارَكَ وتَعالَى مِنهُ

"Mount these animals soundly and look after them properly and do not treat them as chairs for your conversations in the streets and the markets, for many riding animals are better than their rider and are more remembering of God – Blessed and most High". [55]

As mentioned, the crown of creation and the chosen vicegerent of God on earth is the human being. The Qurān commands Muslims to treat all people, irrespective of color or creed, with dignity. Every human being that roams the earth is from the progeny of Prophet Adam (a.s.), making them all the children of an honorable prophet of God.

---

[54] Kanz al-ʿUmmāl, no. 9051
[55] Kanz al-ʿUmmāl, no. 24957

What should be the guiding principle in governing human interaction? Suffice as an answer are the noble words of the Commander of the Faithful Alī ibn Abī Tālib (a.s.) who once said,

ان الناس صنفان: إما أخ لك في الدين أو نظير لك في الخلق

"People are of two [types] either your brother in faith, or your equal in humanity." [56]

Association and Denouncement

One of the most fundamental aspects of faith is expressing love and veneration for God's righteous servants, and denouncing the wicked and corrupt. The Holy Qurān regards this act as one of the keys of Paradise as God Almighty says,

لا تَجِدُ قَوماً يُؤمِنونَ بِاللَّهِ وَاليَومِ الآخِرِ يُوادّونَ مَن حادَّ اللَّهَ وَرَسولَهُ وَلَو كانوا آباءَهُم أَو أَبناءَهُم أَو إِخوانَهُم أَو عَشيرَتَهُم

"You will not find a people believing in God and the Last Day endearing those who oppose God and His Messenger even though they were their own parents, or children, or brothers, or kinsfolk." [57]

This verse was reportedly revealed at a time in which Muslims fought in battle against their own family members for the sake of protecting Islam.

---

[56] Nahj al-Balāgha Letter 53
[57] Qurān 58:22

49

Beyond this specific instance, the verse indicates that the bond of faith and belief overrides that of family ties and tribal affiliations. It also reflects the broader Qurānic theme that one must not love anything of this world at the expense of one's love for God, His messenger (s.a.) and the Ahlul Bayt (a.s.).

In the famous visitation of Imam Hussain ibn Alī (a.s.) known as Ziyārat Āshūrā, the idea of expressing affinity to the Ahlul Bayt (a.s.) and disavowing their enemies is reinforced:

إِنِّي سِلْمٌ لِمَنْ سالَمَكُمْ، وَحَرْبٌ لِمَنْ حارَبَكُمْ ، وَوَلِيٌّ لِمَنْ والاكُمْ، وَعَدُوٌّ لِمَنْ عاداكُمْ، فَأَسْأَلُ اللهَ الَّذي أَكْرَمَني بِمَعْرِفَتِكُمْ، وَمَعْرِفَةِ أَوْلِيائِكُمْ، وَرَزَقَني الْبَراءَةَ مِنْ أَعْدائِكُمْ، أَنْ يَجْعَلَني مَعَكُمْ فِي الدُّنْيا وَالآخِرَةِ، وَأَنْ يُثَبِّتَ لي عِنْدَكُمْ قَدَمَ صِدْق فِي الدُّنْيا وَالآخِرَةِ

"I am at peace with him who is at peace with you and at war with him who is at war with you; a friend to him who is allied with you and an enemy to him who is an enemy to you. So I beg God, who has honored me to know you and to know your friends and has granted me [the strength and wisdom] to disavow your enemies, to keep me with you in this life and the next and to raise me with you to a lofty station in this life and the next."

Love of the prophets, messengers and imams inspires one to emulate them insofar as they are role models. Additionally, the companions of the prophets, messengers and imams also serve as moral exemplars. In this vein, God says,

قَد كانَت لَكُم أُسوَةٌ حَسَنَةٌ في إِبراهيمَ وَالَّذينَ مَعَه

"There was a good example for you in Abraham and those with him." [58]

---

[58] Qurān 60:4

The duty of every believer towards the Prophet (s.a.), his family and righteous companions is to know them, love them, and subsequently follow their example. Similarly, it is critical to know their opponents and disavow them. As one scholar beautifully put it, "You cannot claim to love Moses without opposing Pharaoh."[59] Therefore, the essence of faith is rejection of falsehood and its promoters, as well as embracement of truth and its supporters.

Truthfulness

One of the most notable virtues in this world, that will hold weight on the Day of Resurrection, is truthfulness. It is the most accurate indicator of piety, even more so than the superfluous prayers and recommended fasts. This is illustrated in the following narration from Imam al- Sādiq (a.s.), wherein he says,

لا تَغْتَرُّوا بِصَلاتِهِم ولا بِصِيامِهِم؛ فَإِنَّ الرَّجُلَ رُبَّما لَهِجَ بِالصَّلاةِ والصَّومِ حَتَّى لَو تَرَكَهُ اسْتَوحَشَ، ولكِنِ اخْتَبِرُوهُم عِندَ صِدقِ الحَديثِ وأداءِ الأمانَةِ

"Do not be deceived by their [lengthy] prayer or their [abundant] fasting, for verily it may be that a man becomes so attached to his prayer and his fasting that were he to stop doing them, he would be greatly disturbed. Rather test these people through the truth in their speech and the prompt return of goods entrusted in their care." [60]

[59] Personal communication, Madrassah al-Balaghi, 2014
[60] al-Kāfī, v. 2, p. 104

The Holy Qurān asserts that the truthful will attain salvation on the Day of Judgment and will be granted Paradise as a recompense for their honesty:

قَالَ اللَّهُ هَذَا يَوْمُ يَنْفَعُ الصَّادِقِينَ صِدْقُهُمْ ۚ لَهُمْ جَنَّاتٌ تَجْرِي مِن تَحْتِهَا الْأَنْهَارُ خَالِدِينَ فِيهَا أَبَدًا ۚ رَضِيَ اللَّهُ عَنْهُمْ وَرَضُوا عَنْهُ ۚ ذَٰلِكَ الْفَوْزُ الْعَظِيمُ

"God will say, 'This day truthfulness shall benefit the truthful. For them there will be gardens with streams running in them, to remain in them forever. God is pleased with them and they are pleased with Him. That is the great success'." [61]

The reward for truthfulness is said to apply only to those who embodied this quality in their earthly lives, when it was a matter of choice. This reward is amplified when the truth is spoken even if it threatens one's interests. Anyone can speak truth when it is advantageous but it takes a person of great integrity to utter the truth even when it leads to one's detriment. In the following tradition, Imam Alī (a.s.) summarizes the true essence of faith as being linked to the virtue of truthfulness when he says,

الإِيمانُ أَن تُؤثِرَ الصِّدقَ حَيثُ يَضُرُّكَ، عَلَى الكِذبِ حَيثُ يَنفَعُكَ

"Faith is to prefer to tell the truth, even if it be to your detriment, over lying, even though it be to your benefit." [62]

Charity

One of the most dangerous spiritual diseases is obsession with the material world. Islamic mystics often warn that one must

---

[61] Qurān 5:119
[62] Nahj al-Balāgha, maxim 458

"live in the world but not allow the world to live within you."
The root of all sin can be traced back to attachment to the
temporal world and its allurements. In a well-known tradition,
Imam al- Sādiq (a.s.) speaks of the vice of loving the worldly
life:

رأسُ كلِّ خطيئةٍ حُبُّ الدُّنيا

"The fountainhead of all sin is the love of this world." [63]

One of the most effective ways to prevent the heart from
becoming engrossed by the iridescent glitter of the material
world is to develop the habit of giving charity. Interestingly,
when the Holy Qurān describes the believers as those who
establish prayers, it typically pairs ritual prayer with charity.
For instance, God Almighty says,

إِنَّ الَّذِينَ آمَنُواْ وَعَمِلُواْ الصَّالِحَاتِ وَأَقَامُواْ الصَّلاَةَ وَآتَوُاْ الزَّكَاةَ لَهُمْ أَجْرُهُمْ عِندَ
رَبِّهِمْ وَلاَ خَوْفٌ عَلَيْهِمْ وَلاَ هُمْ يَحْزَنُونَ

*"Indeed those who have faith, do righteous deeds, maintain
the prayer and give the charity, they shall have their reward
near their Lord, and they will have no fear, nor will they
grieve."* [64]

وَالْمُؤْمِنُونَ يُؤْمِنُونَ بِمَا أُنزِلَ إِلَيكَ وَمَا أُنزِلَ مِن قَبْلِكَ وَالْمُقِيمِينَ الصَّلاَةَ
وَالْمُؤْتُونَ الزَّكَاةَ

*"...and the faithful, they believe in what has been sent down to
you, and what was sent down before you—those who maintain
the prayer, give charity, and believe in God and the Last Day*

---

[63] al-Kāfī, v. 2, p.315
[64] Qurān 2:277

—them We shall give a great reward." [65]

In these two verses, prayer is mentioned alongside charity. The word زَكَاة literally means "purification" and indicates one of the effects of giving charity in that it purifies the heart from the vices of greed and worldly attachment. The Qurān seems to suggest that prayer alone is not a sufficient pathway to God if performed alone. In order to ascend towards God, both prayer and charity must be performed in parallel; the former representing God's right over man, and the latter representing the rights of people.

The act of charity is so sacred in the Islamic tradition that when Imam al- Sādiq (a.s.) would give charity, he would kiss his own hands. When asked about this, he explained,

إِنَّ اللهَ تَبَارَكَ وتَعَالَى يَقُولُ: مَا مِن شَيءٍ إِلَّا وقَد وَكَّلتُ مَن يَقبِضُهُ غَيرِي، إِلَّا الصَّدَقَةَ؛ فَإِنِّي أَتَلَقَّفُها بِيَدِي تَلَقُّفاً

"'Verily God, Blessed and most High, says, 'In My stead, I have entrusted everything to the one who grasps it, except for charity, for verily I immediately seize that up in My Hand'." [66]

This narration indicates that the hand that gives charity is so blessed that it meets the metaphorical hand of God before it reaches its intended recipient.

---

[65] Qurān 4:162
[66] Bihār al-Anwār, v. 96, p.134

Purification of the Soul

One of the primary duties of the Holy Prophet (s.a.) was to teach people how to purify their hearts and souls.

God Almighty lists the sacred responsibilities of His messenger in the following verse:

لَقَد مَنَّ اللَّهُ عَلَى الْمُؤمِنِينَ إِذ بَعَثَ فِيهِم رَسولًا مِن أَنفُسِهِم يَتلو عَلَيهِم آياتِهِ وَيُزَكِّيهِم وَيُعَلِّمُهُمُ الكِتابَ وَالحِكمَةَ وَإِن كانوا مِن قَبلُ لَفي ضَلالٍ مُبينٍ

"God certainly favored the believers when He raised up among them a messenger from among themselves to recite to them His signs and to purify them, and to teach them the Book and wisdom, and earlier they had indeed been in manifest error." [67]

The Holy Prophet (s.a.) was a roaming spiritual physician who specialized in curing hearts from dangerous vices. Imam Alī (a.s.) describes the Prophet (s.a.) as such when he says,

طبيبٌ دَوَّارٌ بِطِبِهِ، قَد أَحكَمَ مَراهِمَهُ، وأحمى مَواسِمَهُ، يَضعُ ذَلِكَ حيثُ الحاجةِ إليهِ مِن قُلوبٍ عُميٍ، وآذانٍ صُمٍ، وألسنةٍ بُكمٍ.. مُتَتَبِّعٌ بِدوائِهِ مواضِعَ الغَفلةِ، ومواطِنِ الحَيرةِ

"The Prophet was like a roaming physician who has set ready his ointments and heated his instruments. He uses them wherever the need arises for curing blind hearts, deaf ears,

---

[67] Qurān 3:164

55

and dumb tongues. He targeted with his medicines, negligence and perplexity." [68]

One of the central themes of the Qurān is the purification of the human soul. In Surat al-Shams, God swears by seven things, the last of which is the human soul and declares that the successful ones are those who purify it:

وَنَفْسٍ وَمَا سَوَّاهَا فَأَلْهَمَهَا فُجُورَهَا وَتَقْوَاهَا قَدْ أَفْلَحَ مَن زَكَّاهَا وَقَدْ خَابَ مَن دَسَّاهَا

"...by the soul and Him who fashioned it, and inspired it with [discernment between] its virtues and vices. Indeed, he prospers who purifies it. Indeed he fails who obscures it." [69]

These verses have served as the inspiration for extensive literature on the purification of the soul, which some argue is the entire purpose of the Qurān. One may reasonably extend this to the prophetic mission, as it is reported that the Holy Prophet (s.a.) said,

إِنَّمَا بُعِثْتُ لِأُتَمِّمَ مَكَارِمَ الْأَخْلَاقِ

"Verily, I have been sent [by God] to perfect noble character." [70]

Muslim ethicists draw an important distinction between noble character and good character in the following manner:

---

[68] Nahj al-Balāgha, sermon 108
[69] Qurān 91:7-10
[70] Makārim al-Akhlāq, p. 8

1. محاسن الاخلاق - Good character is to reciprocate goodness. For instance, it is to show kindness towards those who have been kind to you.
2. مكارم الأخلاق - Noble character is to repel evil with goodness. For example, it is to show mercy to the one who once oppressed you when you have the upper hand.

When Imam al- Sādiq (a.s.) was asked to explain the meaning of 'noble character', he replied saying,

العَفوُ عَمَّن ظَلَمَكَ، وصِلَةُ مَن قَطَعَكَ، وإعطاءُ مَن حَرمَكَ، وقَولُ الحقِّ ولَو علَى نَفسِكَ

"Pardoning someone who has oppressed you, repairing broken ties, giving to the one who has deprived you, and speaking the truth even if it is against yourself." [71]

Thus, the Holy Prophet (s.a.) was sent to teach humanity the highest moral virtues and cleanse their hearts from detestable traits. His aim was to make morality and nobility second nature whereby goodness flows from the heart naturally and without internal resistance. When the heart achieves purity, it will become a mirror that will reflect the 99 names of God and thus attain the true station of being God's vicegerent on earth.

---

[71] Ma`ani al-Akhbār, p. 191

Chapter Three: Material Blessings of Paradise

A meticulous perusal of the Holy Qurān and the narrations of the Ahlul Bayt (a.s.), reveal that resurrection is both a spiritual and bodily experience. The Hour of Resurrection is described in the Qurān as a reunion of the body and soul. God Almighty declares:

وَإِذَا النُّفُوسُ زُوِّجَت

"And when souls are reunited [with their bodies]." [72]

Consequently, both reward and punishment target the two dimensions of man, the body and the soul, the material and the immaterial. There are chastisements in the hereafter that inflict pain on the soul, such as being barred from directly addressing God, while other forms of torment are aimed towards the body, such as the consumption of scalding water. Similarly, the rewards of Paradise cater to the soul as well as the body. There are some pleasures that are sensual and bodily in their nature, such as the adornment of silk garments and the diverse array of foods, while others satisfy the more sophisticated needs and wants of the soul, such as tranquility and enjoying intense nearness to God, which is considered the

---

[72] Qurān 81:7

source of all goodness.

In this chapter, we will explore the various material blessings and carnal delights mentioned throughout the Holy Qurān. The following are approximately 14 material blessings explicitly mentioned throughout the Holy Qurān:

1. The gardens and rivers
2. The ample shade
3. The palaces
4. The furniture
5. The food
6. The pure drinks
7. The best drink
8. The dishware
9. The garments
10. The jewelry
11. The maidens
12. The servants
13. The hosts
14. The incomprehensible delights

Gardens and Rivers

وَمَن يُطِعِ اللَّهَ وَرَسُولَهُ يُدْخِلْهُ جَنَّاتٍ تَجري مِن تَحتِهَا الأَنهَارُ خَالِدينَ فيهَا ۚ وَذَلِكَ الفَوزُ العَظيمُ

"...and whoever obeys Allah and His Messenger, He shall admit him to gardens with rivers running in them, to remain in them [forever]. That is the great success." [73]

---

[73] Qurān 4:13

Gardens with rivers running through them are one of the most common features of Paradise in the Qurān. The Qurān depicts Paradise as a vast collection of gardens, vineyards and orchards unlike anything seen in the earthly world. Perhaps the closest word in any human language that can help us appreciate the reality of Paradise, is the word 'garden' or جنة as it is translated in classical Arabic. It is important to consider the etymology of the word جنة. The Holy Qurān uses various derivatives of the word جنة to describe the gardens of Paradise. The word جنة and its derivatives جنات، جنتان، جنان all share the same three-letter root جَنّ which literally means to hide or conceal. The following Arabic words all share the same three-letter root and all relate to the idea of something being hidden or concealed from the naked eye.

1. جنة: is an Arabic word which means 'garden'. The ancient Arabs employed this word to describe a garden because the branches of trees and dense vegetation would cover and conceal the ground if one was to look at the ground from above. Since the word جَنّ literally means to hide and conceal, the Arabs deemed this word to be appropriate to describe a garden.

2. جنين: is an Arabic word which refers to a fetus in the womb of its mother. Since the fetus cannot be seen and is essentially hidden from our eyes, the Arabs used the word جنين to point to an unborn fetus. Notice that this word also contains the three-letter root جَنّ.

3. جن: is an Arabic word which refers to Jinn. Jinn are supernatural creatures but are not perceptible to the human eye.

4. جنون: is an Arabic word which refers to the state of insanity. An insane person acts as though his intellect is hidden or concealed, hence the usage of the same three-letter root.

63

It is noteworthy to mention, that the description of a Paradise of gardens and rivers has attracted sharp criticism from orientalists, who contend that such a Paradise is appealing to the desert dwelling Arabs and serves as convincing evidence that the Qurān was written by a desert Arab of the 7th century. Skeptics argue that since a desert is void of vegetation and water, it only makes sense that in the mind of the Arabs, Paradise would be a place of greenery and flowing water. Modern psychology has established that it is in our base nature as human beings to be drawn to vegetation[74] and water[75]. Greenery and water are not only appealing to those who spend their lives in the barren deserts, rather they make up the landscape of the overwhelming majority of popular vacation destinations. A simple internet search of the most exotic retreat spots around the world will generate countless images of greenery and water.

In Surat al-Rahmān there are two descriptions given of the gardens of Paradise. The first depicts the gardens of the upper levels of Paradise, while the second refers to the gardens of the lower levels. Of the gardens of the higher stations, the Qurān says,

ذَوَاتَا أَفْنَانٍ

"Both abounding in green branches." [76]

---

[74] Burton, E. J., Mitchell, L. & Stride, C. B. (2011). *Good places for aging in place: development of objective built environment measures for investigating links with older people's wellbeing.* BMC Public Health, 11, 839.

[75] Nichols, W. J. (2014). *Blue mind: the surprising science that shows how being near, in, on or underwater, can make you happier, healthier, more connected and better at what you do.* New York: Little, Brown and Company.

[76] Qurān 55:48

64

According to some commentators, these first two gardens are for the foremost in faith who are identified in the Qurān as those enjoy a unique nearness to God. It may seem peculiar to use the word "branches" to describe a garden. One would reasonably assume that words like 'colorful flowers', 'exotic fruits', or 'lush green leaves' would be used instead. However, in the Arabic language, this is a common rhetorical device whereby something trivial is described in order to leave that which is more significant to the imagination. For instance, if one was to visit a grand palace, the likes of which no one has seen, upon being asked to describe the luxuries, such a person may say, "Even the door knobs were made of the finest gold", whereby something trivial is described to convey the unparalleled splendor of that palace. Since Paradise is beyond the reach of human comprehension, the finest detail of the garden is mentioned to allow the human mind to speculate about the rest of this wondrous place. The mentioning of "green branches" also denotes branches that bear fruit and leaves providing both shade and nourishment. The word أفنانٍ could also be read as a plural of فَن, meaning 'sort' or 'variety', thus indicating a host of trees and fruits.

Of the lower gardens of Paradise, the Qurān asserts:

مُدهامَّتانِ

"Dark green." [77]

Dark green indicates a very dark shade of green due to the density of the vegetation and foliage. This is taken by some to suggest that the ground of these two gardens of the lower levels of Paradise is covered with thick vegetation, while in

---

[77] Qurān 55:64

the upper levels of Paradise, the trees dominate.[78]

These dense gardens are described as having rivers flow through and beneath them. Water is the source of all life, and the rivers of Paradise give life to the lush gardens while guaranteeing its continual freshness. Its flowing waters are not only a source of delight for the eyes, but also made easily accessible to the denizens of Paradise. One narration offers a telling description of the uniqueness of these rivers:

ان انهار الجنة ليست في اخاديد انما تجري على سطح الجنة منضبطة بالقدرة حيث شاء أهلها

"Verily the rivers of Paradise are not in trenches, rather they flow on the surface of Paradise and [its currents] are governed by the will of its people." [79]

Scientists have also conducted new research on the physical effects we experience when exposed to the colors green and blue. [80] As for green, studies show that the human pituitary gland is stimulated, muscles are more relaxed, and blood histamine levels increase, which leads to a decrease in allergy symptoms and dilated blood vessels, aiding in smoother muscle contractions.[81] In short, green is calming, stress-relieving, and a bit paradoxically invigorating. It has been shown to improve reading ability and creativity.[82]

---

[78] Nasr, H. (2015). *The Study Quran*. New York: Harper Collins
[79] Tafsīr al-Qurtubi, v. 1, p. 240
[80] Azeemi, S. T. Y. & Raza, S. M. (2005). A Critical Analysis of Chromotherapy and its Scientific Evolution. *Evidence-Based Complementary and Alternative Medicine*, 2(4), p. 481-488
[81] Ibid.
[82] Ibid.

New research also indicates that the color blue has a calming effect and helps combat fear and anxiety.[83] For instance, many people have a fear of flying. This form of travel is often associated with sickness, discomfort, and chaos. To help combat these negative feelings towards flight, many airlines, such as Continental, AirTran, and JetBlue have incorporated the color blue into their brand identity, designed to suggest security, stability, cleanliness, safety, and peace.[84]

Ample Shade

وَنُدخِلُهُم ظِلًّا ظَلِيلًا

"and We shall admit them into an ample shade."[85]

One of the most important aspects of comfort and relaxation is temperature control and sunlight exposure. We have all experienced the discomfort of the sweltering heat under the rays of the sun. Even the most beautiful of places can turn into a miserable experience if the temperature is too hot and the rays of the sun are unshielded. In addition to the breathtaking scenery of the paradisal garden, the Qurān also makes mention of the blessing of extended and everlasting shade. The shade of this earthly life is temporary and is subject to elongation and contraction as the sun rises and sets. In contrast, the shade of Paradise is cast by the enormous branches of its plentiful trees and is permanent and available for all residents of Paradise.

---

[83] Ibid.
[84] Gani, L., Gitaharie, B. Y., Husodo, Z. A. & Kuncoro, A. (2016). *Competition and Cooperation in Economics and Business*. Rutledge: New York.
[85] Qurān 4:57

أُكُلُها دائِمٌ وَظِلُّها

"its fruits and shade are everlasting." [86]

According to a ḥadīth, the Prophet (s.a.) said, "In the Garden there is a tree in whose shade a rider would travel for a hundred years without the shade being broken." [87] The extended shade in Paradise provides an ideal temperature, neither cold nor hot. The Holy Qurān asserts that one of the benefits of this extended shade is a climate conducive for comfort and relaxation. God Almighty says,

لا يَرَونَ فيها شَمسًا وَلا زَمهَريرًا

"They will find in it neither any [scorching] sun, nor any [biting] cold." [88]

Some commentators contend that 'shade' also denotes covering and shelter, and can be used figuratively to imply 'protection'. It can also indicate a state of ease, pleasure, and abundance. These verses, where the blessing of shade is recounted, are seen by some scholars as an allusion to the eternal security and felicity attained in Paradise. [89]

The Palaces

وَمَساكِنَ طَيِّبَةً في جَنّاتِ عَدنٍ

---

[86] Qurān 13:35
[87] Biḥār al-Anwār, v. 8, p. 134
[88] Qurān 76:13
[89] Nasr, H. (2015). *The Study Quran.* New York: Harper Collins

"and good dwellings in the Gardens of Eden." [90]

The Holy Qurān makes frequent references to the lofty abodes of the people of Paradise, and employs various adjectives when describing their places of dwelling. In the above-mentioned verse, the homes of Paradise are described as طَيِّبَة which broadly denotes goodness and tranquility. It is a place that not only pleases guests but is a source of serenity and calmness for its residents. There are many people who live in the most lavish homes but feel constricted and imprisoned by the four walls of their dwellings, which begs the question, what is the value of a home if it is not pleasing to its owner?

In other verses, the Qurān depicts the lofty abodes as being elevated and raised. God Almighty says,

أُولَٰئِكَ يُجْزَوْنَ الْغُرْفَةَ بِما صَبَرُوا

"Those shall be rewarded with lofty abodes for their patience." [91]

The word غُرْفَة refers to the uppermost part of a dwelling, which is regarded as one of the attractive amenities of Paradise. An elevated living space provides a spectacular view of the stunning landscape, gentle breezes, and a sense of security and protection as the Holy Qurān alludes to when it says,

وَهُم فِي الْغُرُفاتِ آمِنونَ

"...and they will be secure in lofty abodes." [92]

---

[90] Qurān 9:72
[91] Qurān 25:75
[92] Qurān 34:37

Even in our earthly life, one of the key factors in determining the value of residential real estate, in addition to location as a priority, is elevation. In recent years, developers are selling 'peace of mind' by building homes on higher elevations to offer potential buyers impressive views and heightened security.

There are many words in the Arabic language that refer to a living space, but interestingly God Almighty selects the word مساكن, which is derived from the word سكن which literally means 'tranquility' and 'peacefulness'. It is an abode that should be void of negative energy, hostility and spiritual disturbance. From an Islamic perspective, a home is a safe space which offers serenity and peace to its inhabitants. It is a place designated for emotional rest and rejuvenation. The Holy Qurān makes mention of a few things that are intended to offer the human being a sense of peace and tranquility, among which include spouses, the darkness of the night, the supplication of the Holy Prophet (s.a.) for those who pay charity, the tranquility that faith brings about, and our homes.

وَمِن آيَاتِهِ أَن خَلَقَ لَكُم مِن أَنفُسِكُم أَزوَاجًا لِتَسكُنوا إِلَيها

"And of His signs is that He created for you mates from your own selves that you may take comfort in them..." [93]

وَجَعَلَ اللَّيلَ سَكَنًا

"...He has made the night for rest." [94]

إِنَّ صَلاتَكَ سَكَنٌ لَهُم

---

[93] Qurān 30:21
[94] Qurān 6:96

"Indeed your supplication is a comfort to them." [95]

هُوَ الَّذِي أَنْزَلَ السَّكِينَةَ فِي قُلُوبِ المُؤْمِنِينَ

"It is He who sent down tranquility into the hearts of the faithful." [96]

وَاللَّهُ جَعَلَ لَكُم مِن بُيوتِكُم سَكَنًا

"It is God who has made for you your homes as a place of rest." [97]

The Holy Qurān seems to imply that, even in our earthly lives, we must strive to make our homes places of peace, spirituality and composure. In one narration, the Holy Prophet (s.a.) states that a spacious home can bring about prosperity perhaps because of its capacity to host many guests and afford its inhabitants sufficient room to fulfill their needs.

مِن سَعادَةِ المَرءِ المُسلِمِ المَسكَنُ الواسِعُ

The Holy Prophet says, "Part of a Muslim's prosperity is living in spacious housing." [98]

The Furniture

مُتَّكِئِينَ عَلىٰ فُرُشٍ بَطائِنُها مِن إِستَبرَقٍ

---

[95] Qurān 9:103
[96] Qurān 48:4
[97] Qurān 16:80
[98] al-Kāfī, v. 6, p. 526

"[They are] reclining on mattresses whose inner-linings are of silk brocade." [99]

There is a saying that goes, 'The furniture in a home is like the meat and potatoes of a meal'. Furniture takes up the bulk of living space and helps make a home feel occupied, welcoming and complete. There are seven terms used throughout the Holy Qurān to describe the lavish furnishings of Paradise:

1. فراش - mattress
2. سرير - throne
3. أريكة - canopied sofa
4. رفرف - fine fabric cushions
5. عبقري - fine fabric
6. نمرقة - pillows
7. زربية - fine rug

Of the mattresses of Paradise, the Holy Qurān offers a seemingly unusual description when it says,

مُتَّكِئِينَ عَلَىٰ فُرُشٍ بَطَائِنُها مِن إِستَبرَقٍ

"[They are] reclining on mattresses whose inner-linings are of silk brocade." [100]

When assessing the value of a piece of furniture, attention is usually given to its exterior because the exterior is what is visible. However, in this verse, God describes the inner lining of the mattress as being embroidered with rich brocade made of silk and gold. Many Qurānic exegeses comment on this verse with a sense of wonderment and amazement, remarking,

[99] Qurān 55:54
[100] Qurān 55:54

72

"If this is the interior, then what about the exterior?". In one hadīth, the Holy Prophet describes the exterior when he says,

ظواهرها نور يتلألأ

"Its exterior is glimmering light." [101]

The verse also makes mention of the way the people of Paradise sit on their furniture. They are not standing, nor are they sitting, but rather they are reclining. Reclining upon mattresses, is seen as an allusion to being content and at peace. It is regarded as the ultimate posture of relaxation and leisure.

The word سرير and its derivatives occur five times in the Qurān as a type of throne that is designated for public gatherings. In one verse the Qurān asserts,

عَلىٰ سُرُرٍ مَوضونَةٍ مُتَّكِئِينَ عَلَيها مُتَقابِلِينَ

"On embroidered thrones reclining on them, face to face." [102]

"Embroidered" is here interpreted to mean that the thrones are encrusted with gold, pearls and rubies. "Face to face" implies that there is a social aspect to the setting, whereby believers can exchange pleasantries and engage in rich conversation. It can also indicate that none shall need to sit behind another since all will be equally exalted and dignified. In another verse, these thrones are said to be elevated and raised as a sign of great distinction and glory[103]. God Almighty says,

فيها سُرُرٌ مَرفوعَةٌ

---

[101] Tafsīr al-Qurtubi, v. 9, p. 349
[102] Qurān 56:15-16
[103] Nasr, H. (2015). *The Study Quran*. New York: Harper Collins

"...and in it there are raised thrones." [104]

The word أريكة and its derivatives are referenced five times in the Qurān and denote a type of canopied sofa that is used for private and intimate gatherings, presumably with one's spouse. A canopied sofa is a type of seat draped with a curtain that provides ample privacy and shields from the rays of the sun. The Holy Qurān says,

هُم وَأَزْواجُهُم في ظِلالٍ عَلَى الأَرائِكِ مُتَّكِئونَ

"...they and their spouses, reclining on canopied sofas in the shades." [105]

مُتَّكِئينَ فيها عَلَى الأَرائِكِ ۖ لا يَرَوْنَ فيها شَمْسًا وَلا زَمْهَريرًا

"...reclining therein on canopied sofas. They will find in it neither any [scorching] sun, nor any [biting] cold." [106]

When the Qurān speaks of سُرُر, meaning thrones, it mentions it in the context of a social gathering in the presence of other believers facing one another. When الأَرائِك, translated as canopied sofas, are referenced, they are mentioned in the context of an intimate gathering with spouses and mates. It is noteworthy to point out that furniture for public and private gatherings are both mentioned five times each, which may imply the importance of striking a balance between one's private life and one's public life.

No bed, throne, sofa or couch is complete without comfortable cushions and pillows.

---

[104]   Qurān 88:13
[105]   Qurān 36:56
[106]   Qurān 76:13

The Holy Qurān makes mention of these opulent cushions in Surat al-Rahman and Surat al-Ghashiya when it says,

مُتَّكِئِينَ عَلَىٰ رَفْرَفٍ خُضْرٍ وَعَبْقَرِيٍّ حِسَانٍ

"Reclining on fine green cushions and beautiful wonders." [107]

وَنَمَارِقُ مَصْفُوفَةٌ

"...and pillows laid out in an array." [108]

The نمرقة, or pillows being "laid out in an array", indicates that they are always arranged and orderly and that the inhabitants of Paradise are not required to expend any energy on upkeep. Even after use, the pillows remain in perfect order as though they are untouched. The رَفْرَفٍ, or fine cushions, indicate thickly brocaded cushions or fabric that can be found wherever the denizens of Paradise desire. The verse can also be understood as a metaphor for perpetual ease and everlasting comfort. The word عَبْقَرِيّ is typically translated as 'genius' in colloquial Arabic, however in ancient Arab folklore it referred to the mythical land of jinn and is employed as an appellation for anything displaying great mastery and exquisite beauty, or anything that is deemed to be beyond human grasp. [109]

Thus, the Qurān routinely reminds its reader that the delights and comforts of Paradise are so unfathomable, that even its cushions are unlike anything that can possibly be appreciated. All Qurānic depictions of Paradise are intended to give readers a narrow window into a realm of limitless pleasure and joy.

---

[107] Qurān 55:76
[108] Qurān 88:15
[109] Nasr, H. (2015). *The Study Quran*. New York: Harper Collins.

Of the fine rugs and carpets of Paradise, the Qurān uses the word زربية, which according to some linguists, refers to a type of rug that contains a brilliant array of vivid colors that dazzles its beholder. The Qurān says,

$$وَزَرَابِيُّ مَبْثُوثَةٌ$$

"...and fine rugs spread out." [110]

The Qurān asserts that these fine rugs are spread out and are ubiquitous in Paradise. Fine rugs brighten up a room and give warmth and comfort for those who walk, sit and sometimes lie on them. Thus, these rugs offer enjoyment to both the sense of sight and touch, and serve as yet another coveted amenity of Paradise.

The Food

$$وَأَمْدَدْنَاهُم بِفَاكِهَةٍ وَلَحْمٍ مِمَّا يَشْتَهُونَ$$

"We will provide them with fruits and meat, such as they desire." [111]

According to a recent survey that looked at how much time we spend performing daily activities over the course of a lifetime, the average person eats three to five meals per day[112] which amounts to approximately six years of one's lifespan.

---

[110] Qurān 88:16
[111] Qurān 52:22
[112] Bureau of Labor Statistics. (2017). Economics News Release, Table 12, Average hours per day spent in primary activities for the civilian population, 2016 quarterly and annual averages. Retrieved from https://www.bls.gov/news.release/atus.t12.htm.

It should come as no surprise that food consumption is an integral part of the human experience. It has the power to nourish our bodies and impact our emotions. "Let food be thy medicine and medicine be thy food", was the famous slogan of Hippocrates, the ancient Greek physician. The Holy Qurān, incidentally speaks at length about the centrality of food in the paradisal experience. One of the great pleasures of Paradise as recounted by the Qurān is the vast assortment of delicious foods. As a general rule of thumb, the Holy Qurān asserts that the denizens of Paradise shall be provided with any type of food they desire:

لَهُم ما يَشاءونَ فيها وَلَدَينا مَزيدٌ

"There they will have whatever they wish, and with Us there is yet more." [113]

Of the food of Paradise, fruit appears to reign supreme. The overwhelming majority of verses that deal with the food options of Paradise, cast fruit as the main entrée.

في سِدرٍ مَخضودٍ وَطَلحٍ مَنضودٍ

"Among thornless lote-trees. And clustered plantains." [114]

The lote trees of this earthly life have thorns and scarce fruits, whereas in the paradisal gardens they are said to be void of thorns and bear plentiful fruits. The word مَخضود is also understood by some to refer to the sheer quantity of fruits that hang from the tree, implying that they almost touch the ground. [115]

---

[113] Qurān 50:35
[114] Qurān 56:28-29
[115] Nasr, H. (2015). *The Study Quran.* New York: Harper Collins

The term مَنضُودٍ indicates fruit that covers a tree from top to bottom and is so dense that the trunk of the tree is no longer visible[116]. In Surat al-Rahmān there is a subtle distinction made between the food of the upper level of Paradise and the lower stations. Of the lower degrees of Paradise, the Qurān asserts,

فِيهِمَا فَاكِهَةٌ وَنَخْلٌ وَرُمَانٌ

"In both will be fruits, date-palms and pomegranates." [117]

Some commentators of the Qurān contend that this verse means that the fruits of the two lower gardens are more limited than those of the higher gardens, in which there were pairs or two kinds of every fruit. In this verse a list is given and a list usually denotes limited options. "Date-palms" and "pomegranates" are said to be specified because the former is particularly nutritious while the latter has powerful medicinal properties[118]. Those, along with the fig and the olive, are also considered fruits given to human beings here on earth that still retain something of their paradisal quality[119]. Of the higher stations of Paradise, the Qurān does not provide a list but rather suggests a wider selection of foods when it says,

فِيهِمَا مِن كُلِّ فَاكِهَةٍ زَوجانِ

"In both will be two kinds of every fruit." [120]

'Two kinds' translates as زَوجانِ, which can also mean 'varieties' or 'pairs'. Some have interpreted this to mean that one kind of fruit is familiar while one is not.

---

[116] Ibid.
[117] Qurān 55:68
[118] Nasr, H. (2015). *The Study Quran*. New York: Harper Collins
[119] Ibid.
[120] Qurān 55:52

78

The idea of some foods in Paradise bearing resemblance to earthy food, is alluded to when the Qurān quotes a conversation among the believers in Paradise:

كُلَّمَا رُزِقُوا مِنها مِن ثَمَرَةٍ رِزقًا ٢قالوا هٰذَا الَّذِي رُزِقنا مِن قَبلُ ٢وَأُتوا بِهِ مُتَشابِهًا

"...whenever they are provided with their fruit for nourishment, they will say, 'This is what we were provided before', and they were given something resembling it." [121]

Some Qurānic commentators posit that مُتَشابِهًا means 'similarity in appearance with a different taste', or that all the fruits of Paradise are of the highest quality and free from any blemishes as opposed to the fruits on earth. Scholars also point out that it appears that part of the enjoyment of Paradise is found in reminiscing with other believers about the food that was consumed during their earthly experience.

In addition to fruit, the Qurān makes mention of meat as one of the food options of Paradise. The Qurān mentions meat as being among the food of Paradise in only two verses:

وَأَمدَدناهُم بِفاكِهَةٍ وَلَحمٍ مِمّا يَشتَهونَ

"We will provide them with fruits and meat, such as they desire." [122]

وَلَحمِ طَيرٍ مِمّا يَشتَهونَ

"...and meat of fowls as they desire." [123]

[121] Qurān 2:25
[122] Qurān 52:22
[123] Qurān 56:21

79

The minimal mentioning of meat in Paradise, is seen by some as an implicit reminder that we should strive to mimic the diet of the inhabitants of Paradise by limiting meat consumption in our earthly lives. Contrary to popular belief, human beings are argued as not being naturally carnivorous. Marta Zaraska, a prominent Polish-Canadian science journalist writes in her critically acclaimed book *Meathooked: The History and Science of Our 2.5-Million-Year Obsession with Meat*,

> "Vegetarian animals ranging from gorillas to water deer have bigger, sharper canines than we do; our canines aren't specially meant for processing meat. What we lack dentally is more important, in fact, than what we have. Gently open a (calm) dog's jaw, and there at the back will be the carnassial teeth, "blade-like and sharp and perfect for slicing meat." Lions and tigers, raccoons and house cats, all carnivores, have them too. We don't. All the high-quality amino acid proteins we require are readily available in plants."[124]

The fact that the human body can digest and process raw fruits and vegetables but not uncooked meat is another indication that we are herbivorous by nature. The Commander of the Faithful, Alī ibn Abī Ṭālib (a.s.) is reported to have once said:

لا تجعلوا بطونكم مقابر للحيوانات

"Do not make your stomach a graveyard for animals." [125]

---

[124] Zaraska, M. (2016). *Meathooked: The History and Science of Our 2.5-Million-Year Obsession with Meat*. Basic Books, NY
[125] al-Muhajjatul Baydhā, v. 5, p. 156

The Drinks

مَثَلُ الْجَنَّةِ الَّتِي وُعِدَ الْمُتَّقُونَ ﷺ فِيهَا أَنْهَارٌ مِن مَّاءٍ غَيْرِ آسِنٍ وَأَنْهَارٌ مِن لَبَنٍ لَّم يَتَغَيَّرْ طَعْمُهُ وَأَنْهَارٌ مِّنْ خَمْرٍ لَّذَّةٍ لِّلشَّارِبِينَ وَأَنْهَارٌ مِّنْ عَسَلٍ مُّصَفًّى

*"(Here is) a Parable of the Garden which the righteous are
promised: in it are rivers of water incorruptible; rivers of milk
of which the taste never changes; rivers of wine, a joy to those
who drink; and rivers of purified honey."* [126]

There is nothing that compliments a mouthwatering meal like
a refreshing drink. The drinks of Paradise, like its food, are
diverse, delicious, and copious. Many of the drinks in the
paradisal gardens are found in the form of streams and rivers.
The above-mentioned verse speaks of four types of rivers that
flow bountifully through the gardens:

1. Rivers of water - in contrast to the water of this
   earthly life, which becomes discolored and putrid
   with the passing of time, the water of Paradise
   retains its purity and never becomes polluted. This
   is a drink that is said to quench the thirst of the
   dwellers of Paradise.

2. Rivers of milk - the milk of this world spoils and
   becomes sour if not consumed within a given time-
   period, whereas the milk of Paradise remains fresh
   and never expires. This is a drink which is said to
   provide wholesome nourishment to the bodies of
   the people of Paradise.

---

[126] Qurān 47:15

3. Rivers of wine - in contrast to earthly wine which typically induces headaches and leads to intoxication, the wine of Paradise offers all the advantages of wine without its adverse side effects. It is said to be a drink which purifies and revitalizes.

4. Rivers of honey - the Qurān describes the honey of Paradise as being 'pure', which some have understood to mean that it is unlike earthly honey. Earthly honey is made by bees and must then be harvested by experienced bee-keepers, who then thoroughly filter the honey from impurities, such as grains and bee particles. Furthermore, the honey of this world is typically used as an additive, while in Paradise it is a drink created by God and thus is pure and ready for immediate consumption.

Some Islamic mystics interpret the mentioning of these four rivers, as representing four types of Divinely granted knowledge, through which the heart and soul are enlivened and invigorated. They articulate the following:

Water incorruptible is the knowledge that does not change with the defects of delusions, doubt, and differences in corrupt tenets and customary beliefs. And it is for the reverent who have reached the station of the heart. *Milk whose flavor does not change* then represents a lower degree of knowledge that does not change by being mixed with caprice or innovation, the differences between school of law, and the tribalism of those attached to creeds. This is the knowledge pertaining to proper actions that prevents one from acts of obedience and depravity. *The rivers of wine* are then different kinds of love for the Divine

Attributes and the Divine Essence. They are delicious for those who are complete, who have reached the station of witnessing the beauty of the manifestations of the [Divine] Attributes, and directly witnessing the beauty the [Divine] Essence, the ardent lovers who desire Absolute Beauty, in the 'station of the spirit'. And *the rivers of purified honey* are "holy delights" that descend [upon the heart], luminous gleams, and the raptures of realization in states and stations for [spiritual] wayfarers and seekers. Those who drink from the *rivers of purified honey* are thus less numerous than those who drink from *the rivers of wine*, and not everyone who tastes the delight of honey, tastes the sweetness of wine.[127]

The Holy Qurān also speaks of another drink that God has promised the أبرار or 'righteous'. That is, a drink that flows from a spring in Paradise. In Surat al-Insan this pure drink is referenced when it says,

إِنَّ الأَبرَارَ يَشرَبُونَ مِن كَأسٍ كَانَ مِزَاجُها كَافُورًا عَيَنًا يَشرَبُ بِها عِبادُ اللَّهِ يُفَجِّرُونَها تَفجِيرًا

"Indeed, the righteous will drink from a cup seasoned with camphor. A spring where the servants of God drink, which they make to gush forth as they please." [128]

وَيُسقَونَ فِيها كَأسًا كَانَ مِزَاجُها زَنجَبِيلًا عَيَنًا فِيها تُسَمَىٰ سَلسَبِيلًا

"They will be served therein with a cup of a drink seasoned with ginger. A spring in it, named salsabīl." [129]

---

[127] Ta'wil al-Qurān al-Karīm; see 47:15
[128] Qurān 76:5-6
[129] Qurān 76:17-18

وَسَقَاهُم رَبُّهُم شَرَابًا طَهُورًا

"Their Lord will give them to drink a pure drink." [130]

Among the pure drinks of Paradise is a beverage that is seasoned with كافور, translated as camphor, and offered to the pious. In Arabia, camphor was used widely for preparing sweet and savory dishes. It is also thought to have cooling properties and act as a calmative[131]. Some commentators have observed a subtlety in the Quranic text, whereby they note that while the أبرار or righteous, drink of a cup mixed with camphor, عِبَادُ اللَّه, the servants of God, drink directly from a spring that is pure and unmixed. Islamic mystics have purported these drinks to be spiritual symbols, indicating that those who drink what is mixed, are lovers of the Divine Attributes, while the pure spring is for the lovers of the Divine Essence, whose love endures no matter which attributes of God they experience.[132]

The Quran also speaks of a drink mixed with زَنجَبِيل, ginger, which in contrast to camphor, acts as a stimulant. In medieval times, ginger was used as both a spice and a medicine, and among some Arab tribes it was considered a delicacy. The Quran indicates that this ginger mixed drink flows from a spring name سَلسَبِيل, in English, Salsabil, which Arab linguists contend is a compound word comprised of the words سال and سبيل which translate as, "seek a way [to the garden]".[134]

In addition to the mixed drinks, the Quran describes another type of drink known as الشراب الطهور, 'the pure drink', which is

---

[130] Qurān 76:21
[131] Nasr, H. (2015). *The Study Quran*. New York: Harper Collins
[132] Ibid.
[133] Ibid.
[134] Ibid.

given by God to his choicest servants. The word طهور in this context, is an active participle meaning 'purifying'.[135] It is said to be a drink that is not only pure but a purifying agent through which God removes all vice and contamination from the heart. Imam al- Sādiq (a.s) is reported to have described the astounding effect of this drink when he said,

اذا شرب المؤمن الشراب الطهور نسي ما سوى الله وانقطع اليه بالكامل

"When the believer drinks of the pure drink he shall forget all things but God and turn to Him entirely." [136]

The Holy Qurān continues its discussion of the drinks served to the dwellers of Paradise in Surat al-Mutaffifīn when it speaks of pure wine that is sealed with musk. God Almighty says,

يُسقَونَ مِن رَحيقٍ مَختومٍ خِتامُهُ مِسكٌ ۚ وَفي ذٰلِكَ فَليَتَنافَسِ المُتَنافِسونَ

"...as they are served with a sealed wine, whose seal is musk - so for that let the strivers strive." [137]

The word رَحيقٍ refers to a type of pure wine sanctioned by God, that is pure and free from any contaminates. The seal refers either to an actual seal of musk upon the wine, or the scent of musk which is emitted when the end of the wine is reached. Taken literally, the seal ensures that the wine remains impeccably pure, untouched and strictly reserved for the noble servants of God[138]. In describing this pure drink, the Qurān offers a sharp contrast to earthly wine when it says,

---

[135]   Ibid.
[136]   Minhāj al- Sādiqīn, v. 10, p. 110
[137]   Qurān 83:25-26
[138]   Nasr, H. (2015). *The Study Quran*. New York: Harper Collins

بَيْضَاءَ لَذَّةٍ لِلشَّارِبِينَ لَا فِيهَا غَوْلٌ وَلَا هُمْ عَنْهَا يُنْزَفُونَ

*"Snow-white, delicious to the drinkers, wherein there will be
neither headache nor will it cause them intoxication."* [139]

The Best Drink

وَمِزَاجُهُ مِن تَسْنِيمٍ عَيْنًا يَشْرَبُ بِهَا الْمُقَرَّبُونَ

*"...and whose mixture is from Tasnīm, a spring where those
brought near [to God] drink."* [140]

Among all the drinks of Paradise, Qurānic commentators
assert that Tasnīm represents the purest and most supreme
drink of Paradise. Tasnīm is understood by some as a proper
noun with no specific meaning, while others have proposed
that it derives from the verb سَنَمَ, 'to raise', indicating that it
exalts and elevates those who drink it. The Qurān suggests that
there are two main categories of believers in the hereafter: the
companions of the right and those brought near [to God] as
alluded to in Surat al-Wāqi'ah. Tasnīm is understood to be a
spring whose waters are mixed with the pure wine, sealed for
the companions of the right but from which those who are
brought near [to God] drink in its purest form. One narration
confirms this interpretation when it describes the spring of
Tasnīm:

---

[139] Qurān 37:46-47
[140] Qurān 83:27-28

ان اشرف شراب اهل الجنة تاتيهم في عالي تسنيم وهي عين يـشرب بها
المقربون , والمقربون آل محمد والمقربون يشربون من تسنيم بحتا صرفا
وسائر المؤمنين ممزوجا

"Verily, the most noble drink for the inhabitants of Paradise
comes from the peak of Tasnīm, which is a spring from which
the ones brought near [to God] drink, and the near ones are the
household of Muhammad [The Ahlul Bayt]. The ones brought
near [to God] drink from Tasnīm directly and unmixed while
other believers drink of it mixed." [141]

Some commentators assert that Tasnīm is a metaphorical
representation of the knowledge of God, and the rapturous joy
of Divine proximity. Those who are the nearest to God drink
nothing but Tasnīm, for their eyes are fixed upon the
Everlasting Face of God, whereas the rest of the denizens of
Paradise sometimes turn their attention to the pleasures of the
created and sometimes towards God and thus drink a mixture
of Tasnīm. [142]

The Dishware

يُطافُ عَلَيهِم بِصِحافٍ مِن ذَهَبٍ وَأَكوابٍ

"they will be served around with golden trays and goblets."
143

بِأَكوابٍ وَأَباريقَ وَكَأسٍ مِن مَعينٍ

---

[141] Tafsīr Alī ibn Ibrāhīm, v. 2, p. 312
[142] Nasr, H. (2015). *The Study Quran*. New York: Harper Collins
[143] Qurān 43:71

"...with goblets and pitchers and a cup of a clear wine." [144]

وَيُطَافُ عَلَيهِم بِآنِيَةٍ مِن فِضَّةٍ وَأَكوابٍ كانَت قَوارِيرا قَوارِيرَ مِن فِضَّةٍ قَدَّروها تَقديرًا

"They will be served around with vessels of silver and goblets of crystal - crystal of silver [from] which they dispense in a precise measure." [145]

One of the most important principles of fine dining, is food presentation. In the culinary world, it is an established fact that food presentation is just as essential to the success of a dish as its taste and flavor. The outer aesthetics of the food is used to seduce the palate and entice one to take a taste. In several verses, the Qurān makes mention of the dishware upon which the foods and drinks of Paradise are served. The following is a list of the five main Qurānic terms which describe the dishware of Paradise:

1. صِحافٍ - round trays
2. أَكوابٍ - goblets
3. أَباريقَ - pitchers
4. كَأسٍ - cup
5. آنِيَةٌ - vessels

In the first verse, two terms are used to reference the dishware of Paradise. The word صِحافٍ is the plural form of the word صَحْفة which refers to a large round tray designed to carry large quantities of food. The sheer size of the trays, is an indication of the copious food supply readily available at the beckoning

---

of the people of Paradise. The term أكواب is translated as 'goblets' and refers to a fancy cup without a handle, which is typically designed to hold cold beverages. The Qurān describes both as being made of pure gold. In medieval times, gold dishware was sign of prestige and royalty and only the wealthiest could afford it, whereas in Paradise it is the standard dishware for all believers.

The second verse speaks of أباريقَ which refers to "pitchers", and is said to derive from the verb بَرَقَ, meaning 'to shine, glitter, sparkle', and is thus taken to indicate pitchers that glitter and sparkle from their purity.[146] The word كَأس is said to mean, a cup that is filled to the brim, which again points to the unlimited supply of food and drink.

In the last verse, there is a mentioning of the word آنِيَة which translates as 'vessels' and could refer to another type of dishware used to serve food. These vessels are described as being made of silver as opposed to gold which may suggest the variety of the dishware. At the end of the final verse, the Qurān describes the goblets as being made of silver that is transparent like crystal. In one narration, Imam al- Sādiq (a.s.) states,

ينفذالبصر في فضة الجنة كما ينفذ في الزجاج

"The eye can see through the silver in Paradise as it can see through glass."[147]

---

[146] Nasr, H. (2015). *The Study Quran*. New York: Harper Collins
[147] Majma'u al- Bayān, v. 10, p. 410

The Garments

An anthropological study of the early history of human beings reveals that clothing was introduced as a means of protecting the human body against extreme weather conditions in the form of strong winds, intense heat, cold and precipitation. Apart from the practical functions of placing a piece of garment above the skin, wearing clothes also carries specific cultural and social meanings. In Paradise, garments are a symbol of dignity, prestige and nobility. The perfect weather conditions in Paradise suggest that the clothing serves an ornamental function and a means of beautification rather than a means of protection from the elements. Of the garments of Paradise, the Qurān asserts:

وَيَلْبَسونَ ثِيابًا خُضْرًا مِن سُنْدُسٍ وَإِسْتَبْرَقٍ

"...and wear green garments of silk and brocade." [148]

The garments are described as green, because, according to some, this color is the most pleasing to the eye, and signifies vitality, freshness and life. With respect to the fabric of the garments, the Qurān speaks of two main types of fabric; سُنْدُس, silk, and إِسْتَبْرَق, brocade. The word سُنْدُس is said to have Persian origins and refers to the finest, and most expensive silk known to the Arabs. Fine silk garments were regarded as immensely luxurious, particularly in the context of Arabian desert life, where rough woolen garments would have been the norm. [149] Some commentators speculate that these are the garments designated for private life and worn only in the company of one's spouses or intimate mates. The second type

---

[148] Qurān 18:31
[149] Nasr, H. (2015). *The Study Quran.* New York: Harper Collins

of fabric that is mentioned is إِسْتَبرَقٍ, which also has Persian roots, and refers to a thicker silk whose lining is made with rich brocade. Some have postulated that this type of garment is worn by the dwellers of Paradise in public gatherings, and is more suitable for communal settings. The garments of Paradise are so astoundingly opulent and lavish that one narration states:

لو بسط ثوب من اثواب الجنة في الدنيا لاندهش اهلها جميعا

"If a garment from the garments of Paradise were to be sent down to the earth, all of its inhabitants would be in utter awe."
[150]

The Jewelry

Jewelry has been an integral part of human culture, tracing back to the earliest known civilizations. Throughout history, human beings have used jewelry for adornment, as markers of social status, signifiers of affiliation and artistic display.[151] In addition to opulent garments, the Qurān asserts that the beauty of the denizens of Paradise will be further augmented by the finest jewelry. There are three verses in which the jewelry of Paradise is described:

يُحَلَّوْنَ فِيها مِن أَساوِرَ مِن ذَهَبٍ وَلُؤْلُؤًا

"...adorned therein with bracelets of gold and pearl." [152]

---

[150] Rūh al-Ma'ānī, v. 15, p. 249
[151] Trigger, B. G. (1990). Monumental architecture: A thermodynamic explanation of symbolic behavior. *World Archeology, 22*(2), 119-132
[152] Qurān 22:23

يُحَلَّوْنَ فِيها مِنْ أَساوِرَ مِنْ ذَهَبٍ

"...adorned therein with bracelets of gold." [153]

وَحُلُّوا أَساوِرَ مِنْ فِضَّةٍ

"...and they will be adorned with bracelets of silver." [154]

Some commentators contend that these images of fine ornaments and exquisite jewelry suggest that those in Paradise will be like kings basking in eternal grandeur. In virtually every culture, gold is regarded as a precious and treasured commodity but Islamic Law strictly forbids men from enjoying the luxury of wearing gold as a form of jewelry, permitting only women to enjoy it in this earthly life. [155] In the hereafter however, what was once forbidden for men, will become a source of delight. The Holy Qurān does not specify gender when it speaks of the jewelry of Paradise therefore it can be inferred that both men and women will be adorned with dazzling bracelets of gold, silver and pearl. Islamic mystics on the other hand, have interpreted these various luxuries as described in the Qurān as mysterious symbols of spiritual joys of witnessing God in all His Majesty and Beauty. According to them, jewelry signifies splendor and royalty, which point to a manifestation of the Divine Attributes of Kingship and Grandeur.

---

[153] Qurān 18:31
[154] Qurān 76:21
[155] Nasr, H. (2015). *The Study Quran*. New York: Harper Collins

The Spouses and Maidens

The great Greek philosopher Aristotle once said, "Man is by nature a social animal". Human beings are predisposed to seek companionship and perhaps the most important companion is one's life partner and spouse. This is as significant in our earthly lives as it is in Paradise. The Holy Qurān cites the blessing of a loving partner as one of the most joyful aspects of the paradisal experience. Of the spouses in Paradise, the Qurān asserts,

$$\text{وَلَهُم فِيها أَزواجٌ مُطَهَّرَةٌ}$$

"Therein they have spouses made pure." [156]

The spouses of Paradise are said to be مُطَهَّرَةٌ, or purified by God, as opposed to طاهرة, meaning pure, whereby the former indicates a higher degree of purity, and attributes the act of purification to God. The commentators of the Qurān explain the purity of the spouses as meaning that they are free from all forms of ritual impurity, bodily impurity, imperfection and sin. [157] They are said to be physically flawless and spiritually impeccable.

There is a discussion among Qurānic commentators regarding the difference between the believing women in Paradise and the حورالعين, described as wide-eyed maidens. Some say that the two cannot be compared because the latter is a *servant* while the former is *served*. Others explain that believing

---

[156] Qurān 2:25
[157] Nasr, H. (2015). *The Study Qurān.* New York: Harper Collins

women are rewarded in Paradise, while the wide-eyed maidens are part of the reward of Paradise for the believing men. In the following tradition attributed to Imam al- Sādiq (a.s.), the superiority of believing women over the wide-eyed maidens is illustrated when he was asked to expound on the Qurānic verse:

فِيهِنَّ خَيْراتٌ حِسانٌ

"In them (Paradise) are virtuous and beautiful women." [158]

الخيرات الحسان من نساء أهل الدنيا وهن أجمل من الحور العين

The Imam (a.s) explains, "The virtuous and beautiful women are from the [believing] women of the earthly world and they are more beautiful than the wide-eyed maidens". [159]

Some commentators have inferred from the permission granted to men to take up multiple spouses, that it is in the base nature of men to be polygamous and for women to be monogamous. Consequently, the enjoyments in Paradise are fine-tuned to meet the needs and desires of each respective gender.

The word حور العين is invoked frequently throughout the Qurān to describe the beautiful maidens of Paradise. The word حور is the plural form of the word حوراء or أحور which literally means, someone whose white regions of their eyes are extremely white and their pupils are extremely black. This sharp contrast is considered the height of beauty for the eye. Of these wide-eyed maidens, the Qurān offers a number of telling adjectives:

---

[158] Qurān 55:70
[159] Tafsīr Nūr al-Thaqalayn, Sūrah 55 verse 70

$$\text{وَحورٌ عينٌ كَأَمثالِ اللُّؤلُؤِ المَكنونِ}$$

"And wide-eyed maidens, the likeness of concealed pearls."
160

The likening of wide-eyed maidens to concealed pearls indicates both their exquisite beauty and their modest disposition. The Qurān compares their stunning beauty to the most precious jewels of the earthly world when it says:

$$\text{كَأَنَّهُنَّ اليَاقوتُ وَالمَرجان}$$

"As though they were rubies and corals." 161

The maidens of Paradise are said be as pure as rubies and as precious as coral stones, the former pointing to their incredible beauty and the latter referring to their delicate nature. Some commentators have understood the comparison to rubies and corals as a reference to the rosy complexions of these heavenly figures. The following hadīth attributed to the Prophet (s.a.), illustrates the striking beauty of the maidens wherein it says, "If a woman among the women of the inhabitants of Paradise were to look upon the earth, she would fill what is between them with a scent, and all that is between them would become delightful. The veil over her head is better than this world and all that is in it."

The Holy Qurān makes an interesting distinction between the wide-eyed maidens of the higher stations of Paradise and those who occupy the lower levels. Of the wide-eyed maidens of the higher gardens, the Qurān asserts,

---

160 Qurān 56:22-23
161 Qurān 55:57

فِيهِنَّ قَاصِرَاتُ الطَّرْفِ لَمْ يَطْمِثْهُنَّ إِنسٌ قَبْلَهُم وَلَا جَانٌّ

Therein are maidens of modest gaze, whom no human has touched before, nor jinn. " [162]

Whereas the wide-eyed maidens of the lower levels of Paradise are described as:

حُورٌ مَّقْصُورَاتٌ فِي الْخِيَامِ

"Maidens secluded in pavilions". [163]

The distinction is subtle and perhaps undetectable to those who lack proficiency in the Arabic language. The maidens of the higher stations of Paradise are said be to قَاصِرَاتُ الطَّرْفِ, of modest gaze, whereas the maidens of the lower levels are described as مَّقْصُورَاتٌ, secluded. Qurānic commentators note that the maidens of the higher gardens are described with an active participle in Arabic, while those in the lower levels of Paradise are described with the passive participle from the same root قصر [164]. This implies that those of the higher stations are chaste women who willingly restrain their glances and are wholeheartedly committed to their righteous husbands, while those in the lower levels have their glances guarded for them.

The focus on modesty and chastity in the Qurānic portrayals of the women of Paradise speaks to its foundational role in spiritual development. If the women of Paradise are described as chaste and modest, anyone who aspires to be among the denizens of paradisal gardens must strive to acquire this noble

---

[162] Qurān 55:56
[163] Qurān 55:72
[164] Nasr, H. (2015). *The Study Quran*. New York: Harper Collins

trait. Imam Alī (a.s.) highlights the paramount virtue of modesty in the following narration:

زكاة الجمال العفاف

"The zakat of beauty is chastity." [165]

The Servants

وَيَطوفُ عَلَيهِم غِلمانٌ لَهُم كَأَنَّهُم لُؤلُؤٌ مَكنونٌ

"They will be waited upon by youths, their own, as if they were guarded pearls." [166]

The inhabitants of Paradise are said to be served and waited on by youthful servants, who were created for the sole purpose of making the paradisal experience one of optimal comfort and ease. After living a life of devotion to God and service to humanity, the denizens of Paradise are now themselves the served and pampered. To describe the level of service provided to the believers, the Qurān uses the verb يَطوفُ which literally means to circle around something. It is typically used in the context of circumambulating around the Holy Ka'ba, but here denotes the idea that the comfort and ease of the believer is a central concern to these servants and that their service to the people of Paradise is unremitting and unending.

---

[165] Mustadrak al-Wasāil, v. 7, p.46

[166] Qurān 52:24

Other than providing uninterrupted service, these youthful servants, much like the Paradisal maidens mentioned above, exhibit the utmost aesthetic excellence. The Holy Qurān makes mention of this striking beauty and salient nobility, by comparing them to "guarded pearls". In one narration, the Holy Prophet (s.a.) was asked,

يارسول الله الخادم كالوَّلوَّ فكيف المخدوم؟
فقال والذي نفسي بيده ان فضل المخدوم على الخادم كفضل القمر ليلة البدر
على سائر الكواكب

"If the servants are like pearls, how about the [beauty] of those being served?" To which the Prophet replied, "I swear by the One in whose hand is my soul, verily the excellence of the served over the servants is like the excellence of the full moon among the stars." [167]

Of these youthful servants, the Qurān asserts that they are غِلمانٌ لَهُم, which translates as "youth belonging to them". This expression indicates that each believer will be assigned exclusive servants, who never tire or grow weary from serving their masters. In fact, the servants derive great pleasure and enjoyment from catering to the needs of the pious devotees of God.

The Hosts

كُلوا وَاشرَبوا هَنيئًا بِما كُنتُم تَعمَلونَ

---

[167] Tafsīr al-Kashāf; see Sūrah 52:24

"[They will be told:] 'Enjoy your food and drink, [as a reward] for what you used to do'." [168]

There is nothing that makes a gathering more pleasant and enjoyable like the presence of a gracious host. Paradise represents the most noble gathering, whereby the host is the Lord of the Worlds with His legions of angels. Most guests are typically hesitant or too bashful to partake in the amenities and enjoyments available to them. It is the duty of the host to ensure that the guests feel welcomed and comfortable in their new space. The Holy Qurān makes mention of the blessing of gracious hosts who provide hospitality with no reservations:

كُلوا وَاشرَبوا هَنيئًا بِما أَسلَفتُم فِي الأَيّامِ الخاليَةِ

"[He will be told]: 'Enjoy your food and drink, for what you had sent in advance in past days'." [169]

It is unclear who the speaker is in these verses. Is it God speaking to the denizens of Paradise? Is it the angels who are addressing the believers? The identity of the speaker is a subject of debate among Qurānic commentators, but what is beyond doubt, is the incredible hospitality shown to the believers as they settle in their new home - the abode of eternal bliss.

Incomprehensible Delights

---

[168] Qurān 52:19
[169] Qurān 69:24

It is noteworthy to mention, that the material blessings of Paradise are not restricted to the list provided above. As limited beings with finite cognitive abilities, we cannot possibly enumerate the infinite bounties of Paradise, therefore, what has been mentioned thus far is simply a limited portrait of the endless rewards awaiting the righteous servants of God. Human beings are predisposed to crave the infinite and eternal, even during their earthly lives. The soul of man is driven towards unrestricted pleasure and prosperity, and the only realm in which this craving can be satiated is Paradise. In one verse the Holy Qurān affirms this when it says,

$$وَفِيها ما تَشْتَهِيهِ الأَنفُسُ وَتَلَذُّ الأَعيُنُ ۖ وَأَنتُم فيها خالِدونَ$$

"...and therein will be whatever the souls desire and eyes delight in, and you will remain in it [forever]." [170]

Some scholars have said that this verse is the most comprehensive and broad reference to the delights of Paradise. It is reported that Shaykh al-Tabrasī, the prominent Qurānic commentator[171], once said, "If all of creation gathered to produce a description of the blessings of Paradise, they would not be able to add to what has been encompassed by these two [paradisal] characteristics."[172]

When examining the above-mentioned verse, scholars have wondered about the order of the two paradisal adjectives. Why is the delight of the eyes mentioned after the desires of the soul? The following theories have been put forward:

---

[170] Qurān 43:71

[171] Shaykh Abu Alī Fadhl ibn Hasan Tabrasi was a 12th century Persian Shia scholar who died in 548 AH. He is best known for his notable work titled, Majma' al-Bayān fī Tafsīr al-Qurān.

[172] Majma' al-Bayān, v. 9, p. 73

1. The expression ما تَشْتَهِيهِ الأَنفُسُ, or "whatever the souls desire", encompasses all types of pleasure. The Qurān then singles out the pleasure derived from the eyes because it is said that most pleasures begin with the eyes. This is an example of making mention of the specific after the general to highlight its exceptionality.

2. The expression ما تَشْتَهِيهِ الأَنفُسُ, translated as "whatever the souls desire", in this context points to the enjoyments derived from the four senses of touch, smell, taste, and hearing while the phrase وَتَلَذُّ الأَعْيُنُ refers to the gratifications experienced through the vision of the eye. The latter is said to provide a degree of joy that is greater or equivalent to the combination of the other four senses.

3. The expression ما تَشْتَهِيهِ الأَنفُسُ, or "whatever the souls desire", refers to the totality of bodily indulgences while the phrase وَتَلَذُّ الأَعْيُنُ, signifies the spiritual jubilation experienced through the vision of the heart, as it gazes upon majesty and grandeur of the Creator by witnesses the proliferation of His attributes of Perfection.

Paradise is a realm of purity and a domain of great sanctity. The material blessings are only a small aspect of its delights. Paradise is the home of the human soul and its eternal resting place. It is said that human beings do not possess souls, because they are souls, they possess bodies. The body is limited and its enjoyments and pleasures have natural limitations. However, the soul is free from such restrictions and thus craves more lofty forms of gratification. In the next chapter, we will explore the Qurānic verses that shed light on the spiritual blessings of Paradise, which compose the true essence of this eternal abode.

Chapter Four: The Spiritual Blessings of Paradise

Although the human being has a physical reality and a bodily dimension, the true essence of man is spiritual. It is the spirit and soul that give man notable value and great distinction. The Holy Qurān in many verses, makes mention of the creation of Adam. He represented God's crowning creation and commanded all of His angels to bow down in prostration before this new creature. But the question is, when did God command the angels to prostrate before Adam? The answer can be found in the following Qurānic verse:

فَإِذَا سَوَّيْتُهُ وَنَفَخْتُ فِيهِ مِن رُوحِي فَقَعُوا لَهُ سَاجِدِينَ

"And when I have fashioned him completely and breathed into him My spirit, fall down to him in prostration." [173]

The Qurān asserts, that the command to prostrate to Adam came after the spirit was infused into his being, and not prior to that. According to traditions, the spiritless physical body of Adam existed for some time but there was no Divine

---

[173]   Qurān 15:29

105

command to prostrate to him. It was his spiritual potential and his immaculate soul that earned him the lofty station of being God's vicegerent on earth. The human soul is like a child that requires nurturing, discipline and maturation. The earthly world was created precisely for that purpose. Paradise was created to be the final abode for the souls that have traversed the journey of the earthly life, and attained spiritual maturity and enlightenment. It takes an entire lifetime to prime and prepare the soul for the spiritual blessings of Paradise. If there are any deficiencies or faults, God intervenes and cleanses the soul to prepare it for admission into the eternal gardens of bliss. In this chapter, we will embark on an exploratory journey through the verses of the Holy Qurān that offer some descriptions of the spiritual raptures and immaterial enjoyments of Paradise.

Distinct Reverence

The distinct reverence shown to the believers begins even before their official admittance into the eternal gardens of bliss. The Holy Qurān makes mention of the dignified manner in which the righteous are escorted to the gates of Paradise, where they are greeted by angels. The following verse beautifully depicts this grand arrival:

وَسِيقَ الَّذِينَ اتَّقَوْا رَبَّهُمْ إِلَى الْجَنَّةِ زُمَرًا ۖ حَتَّىٰ إِذَا جَاءُوهَا وَفُتِحَتْ أَبْوَابُهَا وَقَالَ لَهُمْ خَزَنَتُهَا سَلَامٌ عَلَيْكُمْ طِبْتُمْ فَادْخُلُوهَا خَالِدِينَ

"Those who are conscious of their Lord will be escorted to Paradise in throngs. When they reach it, and its gates are opened, its keepers will say to them, 'Peace be to you!

106

You are welcome! Enter it to remain [forever]." [174]

In contrast to the wicked who are driven into the Hellfire like debased beasts, the believers are said to be escorted with great honor to the gates of Paradise. Its gates are not closed, nor do they require knocking, but rather, they are opened wide to receive the pious congregants. Among the throngs, the first to enter is said to be a group appearing like the moon on the night when it is full, and they will be followed by a group that looks like the brightest star shining in the sky. The Qurān asserts that people will enter Paradise not as individuals, but as large groups as indicated by the word زُمَرًا. This is intended to instill a sense of community in the hearts of the believers, in order for them to think beyond the limits of the self and strive to develop a God-conscious society. Upon arriving at the gates of Paradise, the angels extend a warm greeting and offer them an impassioned salute for living a virtuous life.

Upon entering the eternal abode, God's angels are commanded to enter Paradise from each gate and greet the new denizens of Paradise. This second greeting from the angels is alluded to in the following verse:

وَالمَلائِكَةُ يَدخُلونَ عَلَيهِم مِن كُلِّ بابٍ سَلامٌ عَلَيكُم بِما صَبَرتُم ۚ فَنِعمَ عُقبَى الدّارِ

"...and the angels will enter upon them from every door. Peace be upon you, for your patience. How excellent is the reward of the [ultimate] abode." [175]

The angels are said to enter from each gate bearing gifts and presents from God to honor the believers. In chapter 5 there will be a detailed discussion of the gates of Paradise, but here it is noteworthy to mention that each gate represents a specific

---

[174] Qurān 39:73
[175] Qurān 13:23-24

righteous act such as "The Gate of Prayer", "The Gate of Fasting", "The Gate of Hajj" etc. The angels will enter from each one of these gates, and congratulate the believers for exhibiting the supreme virtue of patience in their earthly lives. The angels seem to suggest that every virtue is an extension of one of the three types of patience: patience in obedience, patience against sin, and patience in hardship. After praising the believers, the angels remind them that the bounties and delights of this new abode are eternal and everlasting.

In addition to the greetings of the angels, the Qurān speaks of a special greeting and salutation from God himself to the inhabitants of Paradise. This is a greeting of pure love from the Lord of the Worlds as indicated by the following verse:

سَلَامٌ قَوْلًا مِن رَّبٍّ رَّحِيمٍ

"Peace, a word from the all-Merciful Lord." [176]

This Divine greeting will penetrate deep into the souls of the believers, and fill their hearts with complete contentment. It is the greeting that every created being has yearned for from the inception of its existence. It is the climax of all pleasure and the summit of happiness. It is God's seal of approval that brings about an indescribable joy that mutes all other desires. To this effect, it is reported that the Commander of the Faithful, Alī ibn Abī Tālib (a.s.) once said,

لو حجبت عنه ساعة لمت

"If I was veiled from it (God's greeting), I would perish." [177]

---

[176] Qurān 36:58
[177] Tafsīr Rūh al-Ma'āni, v. 7, p. 416

Ambiance of Peace

There is nothing that disturbs the human soul more than an environment of hostility and enmity. It strips away the joy of life and can spoil the most pleasant of gatherings. Antagonism and animosity can transform the most comfortable setting into a miserable prison. For this reason, the Holy Qurān asserts that one of the premier aspects of the paradisal life is the ambiance of peace that fill every space and moment.

لَهُم دارُ السَّلامِ عِندَ رَبِّهِم ۖ وَهُوَ وَلِيُّهُم بِما كانوا يَعمَلونَ

"For them shall be the abode of peace near their Lord and He will be their guardian because of what they used to do."[178]

وَاللَّهُ يَدعو إِلىٰ دارِ السَّلامِ

"God invites to the abode of peace..." [179]

Interestingly, the Qurān assigns دارِ السَّلامِ, which means "Abode of Peace" as one of the names of Paradise. Some have said that this "peace" refers to the complete freedom from pain, hardship, and disorder that were characteristic of the earthly life. The dwellers of Paradise will enjoy a life of prosperity and peace, whereby everyone and everything around them will only heighten the aura of tranquility. Others have said that السَّلامِ, meaning 'Peace' is one of the 99 names of God and Paradise is being attributed to Him, because He is its creator and gracious host. The two views are not mutually

---

[178] Qurān 6:127
[179] Qurān 10:25

109

exclusive and can both be accepted as valid understandings of "The Abode of Peace". However, given the context of these verses, it is more likely that the first opinion represents the more plausible explanation.

In a narration from Ibn Abbās, the prominent companion of the Holy Prophet (s.a.), the meaning of this "Abode of Peace" is Paradise. When asked to explain, he says,

> The Abode of Peace is Paradise. Its inhabitants will be free from all blemishes, imperfections, ailments and sicknesses. They will be rescued from old age, death, and the changing of states. They are the honored who will never be humiliated. They are the prosperous who will never be [struck with] misfortune…They are the living who shall never die. [180]

How will this ambiance of peace be established in Paradise? The following verse offers some insight into how this will be achieved:

وَنَزَعْنَا مَا فِي صُدُورِهِم مِنْ غِلٍّ إِخْوَانًا عَلَىٰ سُرُرٍ مُتَقَابِلِينَ لَا يَمَسُّهُمْ فِيهَا نَصَبٌ وَمَا هُم مِنْهَا بِمُخْرَجِينَ

"We will remove whatever hatred there is in their breasts; [intimate like] brothers, [they will be reclining] on couches, facing one another. Therein neither fatigue shall touch them, nor will they [ever] be expelled from it." [181]

The word غِلّ translates as 'hatred', and in this context, refers to the animosity that existed among the believers during their

[180] Bīhar al-Anwār, v. 8, p. 194
[181] Qurān 15:47-48

earthly life. God is said to remove this resentment from the hearts before admitting anyone into Paradise. The Qurān alludes in many passages that there is no place for hate in Paradise, because it creates internal agitation and external disturbance. Furthermore, the verse highlights, that external peace begins with internal reformation. Even Paradise, with its lush green gardens, flowing rivers, and immaculate dwelling places, cannot be enjoyed unless enmity and rancor are uprooted from the hearts.

Neither Grief nor Fear

Security and safety are among the most underappreciated blessings, and they are often cherished once they are lost. People who live in dangerous cities and unstable regions of the world yearn for nothing more than the establishment of a system that can provide protection from physical and emotional harm. Of the security and safety of Paradise, the Qurān says,

إِنَّ الْمُتَّقِينَ فِي مَقَامٍ أَمِينٍ

"Indeed, the pious will be in a secure place." [182]

The believers will be provided safety from all forms of harm and danger. They will be secure from the assault of Satan, which they were subject to during their earthly lives, and they will be guarded from all worry, fear, terror and grief. The worldly abode was encircled by a constant onslaught of tribulations but now the denizens of Paradise can enjoy absolute security from anything that can inflict injury on their

---

[182] Qurān 44:51

111

bodies or souls.

In another verse, the Qurān asserts that fear and anxiety, which are natural emotions in the earthly world, will be eternally eradicated upon entry into Paradise:

ادخُلُوا الجَنَّةَ لا خَوفٌ عَلَيكُم وَلا أَنتُم تَحزَنونَ

"Enter Paradise! You shall have no fear; nor shall you grieve." [183]

It is said that fear relates to anxiety about the future, while grief relates to pain over a past misfortune. In Paradise however, there are no lurking dangers that would evoke fear nor will its blessings ever be interrupted to give rise to anxiety. Since all human beings have experienced hardship in their past, it is only God who is willing and capable of removing the lingering grief that stings the heart. Some of the most righteous of God's servants can even receive a taste of this in the earthly life. The Qurān makes mention of this blissful state when it says,

أَلا إِنَّ أَولِياءَ اللَّهِ لا خَوفٌ عَلَيهِم وَلا هُم يَحزَنونَ الَّذينَ آمَنوا وَكانوا يَتَّقونَ لَهُمُ
البُشرىٰ فِي الحَياةِ الدُّنيا وَفِي الآخِرَةِ

"Behold! The friends of God will indeed have no fear nor will they grieve. Those who have faith, and are pious. For them is glad tidings in the life of this world and in the Hereafter." [184]

---

[183] Qurān 7:49
[184] Qurān 10:62-64

112

Intimate Friends and Devoted Companions

One of the greatest blessings that God bestows upon the denizens of Paradise, is the company of spiritually elevated friends. The mere presence of these pure and pious companions invigorates the soul and enlivens the heart. They are the honored friends of God who speak nothing but wisdom and emanate nothing but love. A single interaction with them eclipses all the pleasures of the temporal world. They are the most noble of friends and the most distinguished of acquaintances. Of the blessings of righteous company, the Qurān asserts,

وَمَن يُطِعِ اللَّهَ وَالرَّسُولَ فَأُولَٰئِكَ مَعَ الَّذِينَ أَنْعَمَ اللَّهُ عَلَيْهِم مِنَ النَّبِيِّينَ وَالصِّدِّيقِينَ وَالشُّهَدَاءِ وَالصَّالِحِينَ ۚ وَحَسُنَ أُولَٰئِكَ رَفِيقًا ذَٰلِكَ الْفَضْلُ مِنَ اللَّهِ ۚ وَكَفَىٰ بِاللَّهِ عَلِيمًا

Whoever obeys God and the Messenger —they are with those whom God has blessed, including the prophets and the truthful, the martyrs and the righteous, and excellent companions are they! That is the grace of God, and God suffices as knower [of His creatures].[185]

The friends of the dwellers of Paradise are the best of creation. They include the great prophets, the truthful servants of God, the selfless martyrs, and the righteous. In the earthly world, the believers are often compelled to associate with people who bring them misery and grief. No matter how much they try to avoid their company, the circumstances of life dictate that the righteous and the wicked must cross paths. However, in the hereafter, humanity will be separated in accordance to virtue

---

[185] Qurān 4:69-70

113

or lack thereof. The sinful will be grouped with the sinful and the pious will be gathered with the pious.

The following narration illustrates the context of the above-mentioned verse. The verse was reportedly revealed when Thawbān, one of the companions, expressed dismay at the thought of being separated from the Holy Prophet (s.a.) in Paradise. He complained to the Prophet saying,

يا رسول اللّه اذا لم ارك اشتقت اليك واستوحشت وحشة شديدة حتى الـقـاك فذكرت الاخرة فخفت ان لا اراك هناك لاني ان ادخلت الجنة فانت تكون فـي درجات النـبـيـين وانا في درجات العبيد فلا اراك وان انا لم ادخل الجنة فـحـيـنـئذ لااراك ابداً

"O Messenger of God, when I do not see you, I yearn for you and experience an intense loneliness until I meet you. Then I remember the hereafter and fear that I will not see you because if I enter Paradise, you will occupy the station of prophets and I will occupy the station of [average] servants [of God] and thus, will not see you. And if I am not admitted into Paradise, I shall never see you." [186]

After posing this heartfelt grievance to the Holy Prophet (s.a.), the above-mentioned verse was revealed which asserts that the obedient shall earn the noble company of their prophet after death. According to other traditions, the Prophet (s.a.) periodically assured his followers that if they loved God, the Prophet (s.a.) and his immaculate family, they would be with those whom they love in the hereafter, even if there was deficiency in their deeds.

Qurānic commentators have wondered about the sequence of the four groups mentioned, whereby the prophets (a.s.) are

---

[186] Tafsīr Majma' al- Bayān; see Sūrah 4 verse 69

mentioned first, followed by the truthful, the martyrs and the righteous. Some have said that the order reflects the various groups that must rise to the occasion in the face of opposition to the truth. Historically, when God has sought to guide a people, he has dispatched a prophet to begin the process of guidance. After the departure of prophets (a.s.), there was a need for individuals to protect that message through word and deed. These individuals were the truthful ones who guarded the message from distortion and exhibited perfect authenticity between word and action. As the Divine message spread far and wide, so too did the antagonism of God's enemies rise, and they sought to obliterate the Divine word. This is where the need for sacrifice arose, and martyrs gave their lives to ensure the survival of the message and the defeat of its adversaries. After that, the earth is promised to be inherited and ruled by the righteous as God declares,

وَلَقَد كَتَبنا فِي الزَّبورِ مِن بَعدِ الذِّكرِ أَنَّ الأَرضَ يَرِثُها عِبادِيَ الصّالِحونَ

"Certainly We wrote in the Psalms, after the Torah: 'Indeed My righteous servants shall inherit the earth'." [187]

It is important to note that being in the company of messengers, prophets and imams does not equate achieving their status in Paradise. Rather, it indicates the possibility of connecting with them and enjoying their company. God Almighty speaks of the social interactions of Paradise in the following verse:

إِخوانًا عَلىٰ سُرُرٍ مُتَقابِلينَ

"[so they will be] brothers, on thrones facing each other." [188]

---

[187] Qurān 21:105
[188] Qurān 15:47

115

Pleasant Social Interactions

In Paradise, as well as in the earthly life, it is incontestable that pleasant social interactions are significant contributors to human happiness and contentment. The way human beings interact with one another, impacts the way they experience and perceive the world that surrounds them. The Holy Qurān depicts Paradise as a place of mutual respect, completely void of hatred, deceit, falsehood, envy and sinful speech.

لَا يَسْمَعُونَ فِيهَا لَغْوًا وَلَا تَأْثِيمًا إِلَّا قِيلًا سَلَامًا سَلَامَ

"They will not hear therein any vain talk or sinful speech, but only the utterance, 'Peace!' 'Peace!" [189]

It is said that the word لَغْوًا refers to any speech that is devoid of meaning and value, or speech that expresses devious tendencies[190]. The word تَأْثِيمًا indicates that in Paradise, there is no lying or any form of sinful speech. There is no incitement towards anything that can inflict harm upon the souls. Unlike the earthly life, this world is protected from inflammatory speech and hateful rhetoric. The believers will only hear words of peace, enlightenment and truth.

Some commentators have posited that the expression سَلَامًا سَلَامًا is employed here to signify freedom from all evils and defects and absolute inner contentment. Others maintain that this refers to the greeting of peace from God and His angels to the believers.

---

[189] Qurān 56:26-26
[190] Nasr, H. (2015). *The Study Quran.* New York: Harper Collins

There is a common misconception among people that religious folk are dull, humorless and incapable of having a good time. Mark Twain once wrote, "Heaven for climate, Hell for company". However, the Qurān offers a refreshingly different perspective on the inhabitants of Paradise. In one verse it states,

إِنَّ أَصحابَ الجَنَّةِ اليَومَ في شُغُلٍ فاكِهونَ

"Indeed, today the inhabitants of Paradise rejoice in their [playful] engagements" [191]

According to some, one of the meanings of the word فاكِهونَ; is to joke and be endearingly playful. The people of Paradise are described as people of humor and light heartedness. Below are a few narrations that describe the pleasant and lovable nature of a believer:

قال رَسولُ اللهِ صَلَّى اللهُ عَلَيهِ وَآلِهِ: المؤمنُ دَعِبٌ لَعِبٌ، والمُنافِقُ قَطِبٌ غَضِبٌ

The Holy Prophet (s.a.) once said, "A believer is fun and playful and a hypocrite is grim and angry." [192]

قال الإمامُ الباقِرُ عَلَيهِ السَّلامُ: إنَّ اللهَ عَزَّ وجلَّ يُحِبُّ المُداعِبَ في الجَماعةِ بِلا رَفَثٍ

Imam al-Bāqir (a.s.) once said, "Indeed, God loves those who are playful among people without obscenity." [193]

---

[191] Qurān 36:55
[192] Tuhaf al-Uqūl, p.49
[193] Al-Kāfī, v. 2, p. 663

عن يونسَ الشَّيبانيِّ: قال أبو عَبْدُاللهِ عَلَيهِ السَّلامُ: كَيفَ مُداعَبَةُ بَعضِكُم بَعضاً؟
قُلتُ: قَليلٌ، قالَ: فَلا تَفعَلُوا، فَإنَّ المُداعَبَةَ مِن حُسنِ الخُلقِ، وإنَّكَ لَتُدخِلُ بِها
السُّرُورَ عَلَى أخيكَ، ولَقَد كانَ رَسُولُ اللهِ صَلَّى اللهُ عَلَيهِ وَآلِهِ يُداعِبُ الرَّجُلَ يُريدُ
أن يَسُرَّهُ

Imam al- Ṣādiq (a.s.) asked Yūnus al-Shaybānī, 'How much do you joke around with each other?', to which he said, 'Little.' He (a.s.) responded, 'This is not how it should be, for playing is part of good character, and through that you bring happiness to your brother, and the Messenger of God would joke with people wanting to make them happy'".[194]

Inner Peace and Outer Joy

Inner peace is truly the key to human happiness. It is said that if the heart is tranquil, the external environment cannot impact that state of calmness and composure. Without inner peace, no amount of material comfort can remedy the unease. Without a tranquil heart, there is no medicine for the agonizing apprehension.

The joy that the inhabitants of Paradise experience is a natural result of possessing pure hearts, overflowing with Divine love. The jubilation originates from the heart and manifests itself outwardly like a flower that blooms in the spring. The Holy Qurān speaks of this pure joy when it says,

ادخُلُوا الجَنَّةَ أنتُم وَأزواجُكُم تُحبَرونَ

"Enter Paradise, you and your spouses, made joyous." [195]

---

[194] Ibid.
[195] Qurān 43:70

118

The word تُحبَرونَ comes from the root حبر which literally
means, 'to leave a beautiful impression'. The idea here being
that when someone is joyous, they also beautify and enhance
the lives of those around them. Joyous people bring joy to
others.

In another verse, this uncontainable happiness is described:

تَعرِفُ في وُجوهِهِم نَضرَةَ النَّعيمِ

"You will perceive in their faces the freshness of bliss." [196]

The blessings of Paradise, both physical and spiritual, are so
overwhelming that it is virtually impossible to conceal the
exhilaration. The splendor of cheerfulness can be recognized
in their faces. In another verse, the Qurān asserts that the joy
actually begins when they receive the news of salvation and
eternal reward.

وُجوهٌ يَومَئِذٍ مُسفِرَةٌ ضاحِكَةٌ مُستَبشِرَةٌ

"Faces that Day shall be shining, radiant, laughing, joyous."
[197]

Some scholars assert that these verses describe the
psychological state of the believers on the Day of resurrection.
Since the face is the mirror of the heart, this external joy is a
manifestation of the happiness of the heart. The faces of the
believers are shining and radiant from the joy they experience
from the glad tidings of God's pleasure and everlasting bliss.

[196] Qurān 83:24
[197] Qurān 80:38-39

God's Pleasure

Love is one of the most powerful human emotions. Universally, people desire to love and to be loved. Throughout history, human beings have marvelled at this phenomenon and made it the central theme of some of the best stories ever told.

One such fable tells the tale of the two lovers, Layla and Majnūn. According to this tale, Qays Ibn al-Mulawwah, who later became known as 'Majnūn', which means 'madman', fell in love with Layla, and began composing passionate poems, expressing his adoration for her and mentioning her name often. His over the top efforts to woo her made some of the locals call him Majnūn. It is said that when he asked for her hand in marriage, her father refused because it would be a scandal to marry a man referred to as mad and mentally imbalanced. Majnūn yearned for nothing more than to be close to his beloved.

A mere glance from her or even a smile of approval, is all that his heart craved. When it became clear to him that he would not marry her, he retreated to the wilderness, where he began writing poems to his Layla.

When news reached Majnūn that Layla had died, he immediately travelled to the place where she had been buried and there he wept and sobbed and uttered these heart-breaking words, words that highlight the pain of being separated from one's true love:

'I pass by these walls, the walls of Layla and kill this wall and that wall. It's not the love of the houses that has taken my heart. But of the one who dwells in those houses.'[198]

This fable illustrates the power of love that exists between two created beings. If this is the love between two human beings, one must wonder, what kind of love should exist between the created and the Creator? Majnūn desired nothing but the pleasure of Layla, for it was the source of his delight. Similarly, the denizens of Paradise see the appeasement of God as representing the most supreme pleasure. The Holy Qurān asserts this notion in the following verse:

وَعَدَ اللّهُ المُؤْمِنِينَ وَالمُؤْمِنَاتِ جَنَّاتٍ تَجْرِي مِن تَحْتِهَا الأَنْهَارُ خَالِدِينَ فِيهَا وَمَسَاكِنَ طَيِّبَةً فِي جَنَّاتِ عَدْنٍ ۚ وَرِضْوَانٌ مِنَ اللّهِ أَكْبَرُ ۚ ذَلِكَ هُوَ الفَوْزُ العَظِيمُ

"God has promised the believers, men and women, gardens with streams running in them, to remain in them [forever], and good dwellings in the Gardens of Eden. Yet God's pleasure is greater [than all these]; that is the great success." [199]

The phrase, "Yet God's pleasure is greater", places the spiritual reward of Divine contentment above all bodily amusements found in the paradisal garden. Some scholars reason that this is because the life of the spirit is greater than the life of the body, while others contend that striving to earn God's approval is superior to striving to earn a reward from Him. In one narration, Imam Alī (a.s.) echoes a similar message when he says,

الجلسة في المسجد خير لي من الجلسة في الجنة، فإنّ الجنة فيها رضى نفسي، والجامع فيه رضىَ ربي

---

[198] *The Story of Layla and Majnun*, tr. by. R. Gelpke (with E. Mattin and G. Hill), Oxford, 1966
[199] Qurān 9:72

"Sitting in a masjid is better to me than sitting in Paradise, because [when I am] in Paradise, I am pleased but in a masjid, God is pleased." [200]

In another tradition, it is reported that God will address the believers in Paradise and offer them the greatest glad tiding. Abū Sa'īd al-Khudrī reports that the Holy Prophet (s.a.) once said,

إن الله يقول لاهل الجنة : يا اهل الجنة , فيقولون لبيك ربنا وسعديك والخير في يديك , فيقول : هل رضيتم فيقولون ومالنا لا نرضى يارب وقد اعطيتنا ما لم تعط احدا من خلقك : فيقول : الا اعطيكم افضل من ذلك , فيقولون يارب واي شي افضل من ذلك فيقول : احل عليكم رضواني فلا اسخط عليكم بعده ابدا

"Verily, God will say to the inhabitants of Paradise, 'O dwellers of Paradise!', to which they will respond, 'Here we are at your service, our Lord, all goodness is in your Hands'. God will then ask, 'Are you pleased?'. [The believers respond in dismay] 'How could we not be pleased O' Lord?! You have given to us what you have not bestowed upon any of your creation'. God responds, 'Shall I give you something even greater [than everything you have already received]?' In meek comprehension and bewilderment, the believers say, 'O' Lord, what is greater than that?' God then proclaims, 'I award you My [good] pleasure after which you shall never experience My wrath!'" [201]

This narration beautifully captures the mutual love between God and the inhabitants of Paradise. He not only rewards them with lavish dwellings, fine garments and delicious food, but assures them that they have earned the ultimate prize, which

[200] Wasāil al- Shīa, v. 5, p. 199
[201] Tafsīr Rūh al-Ma'āni, v. 10, p. 122

is His satisfaction and pleasure. This reciprocal pleasure is highlighted in the following verse:

رَضِيَ اللَّهُ عَنْهُم وَرَضُوا عَنْهُ ۚ ذَٰلِكَ الفَوْزُ العَظِيم

"God is pleased with them and they are pleased with Him. That is the great success." [202]

Al-Rāzi, the prominent Sunni Qurānic commentator, remarks that this mutual contentment, is one of the wondrous secrets of Paradise, whose reality cannot be conveyed through the usage of human speech.[203] It is a joy that can only be understood through experience, not description.

In another verse, God seems to take pride in calling the believers of Paradise, 'His servants'. When addressing a tranquil soul who is departing the earthly life,_He offers the glad tidings of Paradise. God Almighty says,

يا أَيَّتُهَا النَّفسُ المُطْمَئِنَّةُ ارجِعي إِلَىٰ رَبِّكِ راضِيَةً مَرضِيَّةً فَادخُلي في عِبادي وَادخُلي جَنَّتي

"O tranquil soul! Return to your Lord, pleased, pleasing! Then enter among My servants! And enter My Paradise!" [204]

Inner Witnessing and Loving Attention

One of the most valuable spiritual rewards of Paradise is

---

[202] Qurān 5:119
[203] Nasr, H. (2015). *The Study Quran.* New York: Harper Collins
[204] Qurān 89:27-30

witnessing the Lord of the Worlds through the eye of the heart. Since God transcends space and time, and is infinite, it is only possible to see Him, not through eye sight, but rather through insight. It is reported that a man once asked Imam Alī (a.s.) about the possibility of seeing God with one's physical eyes. The following narration showcases the intriguing conversation:

يا أمير المؤمنين هل رأيت ربّك حين عبدته؟
قال: فقال: ويلك ما كنت أعبد رباً لم أره،
قال: وكيف رأيته؟
قال: ويلك لا تدركه العيون في مشاهدة الأبصار ولكن رأته القلوب بحقائق الإيمان

"O Commander of the Faithful, have you seen your Lord when you worship Him?"

The Imam retorted, "Woe be to you, I would not worship a Lord that I cannot see!"

"How did you see him", asked the man.

The Imam clarified, "Eyes do not perceive Him through the witnessing of sight but hearts recognize Him through the realities of faith." [205]

Of this inner-witnessing, the Qurān asserts,

وُجوهٌ يَومَئِذٍ ناضِرَةٌ إِلىٰ رَبِّها ناظِرَةٌ

"Some faces will be radiant on that day, gazing upon their Lord." [206]

---

[205] Al- Kāfī, v. 1, p.98
[206] Qurān 75:22-23

124

Most Sunni commentators take the assertion that believers will be "gazing upon their Lord" as a reference to the literal vision of God in the hereafter. They contend that while the believers are veiled from Him in the earthly world, they will be rewarded with a sort of unveiling which will enable them to see God with their eyes[207]. Shīa scholars, on the other hand, argue that this verse must be understood in the light of Sūrah 6 verse 103, which negates the possibility of perceiving God in the literal sense. Thus, "gazing upon their Lord" is interpreted as a symbolic witnessing of the Divine and the anticipation of His vast mercy. When the believers gaze upon their Lord, His Beauty and Majesty will distract them from the rest of creation. Once their hearts are fixated upon Him, all other things become peripheral, and even if they turn their attention towards others, it is but a fleeting glance.

Conversely, the greatest punishment on the Day of Resurrection, will be God's indifference and disregard for the wicked and sinful. Since they were heedless of Him in their worldly lives, He too will reciprocate by forgetting them when they rise from their graves. God Almighty says,

لَا يُكَلِّمُهُمُ اللَّهُ وَلَا يَنظُرُ إِلَيهِم يَومَ القِيامَةِ وَلَا يُزَكِّيهِم وَلَهُم عَذابٌ أَليمٌ

"and God will not speak to them nor will He [so much as] look at them on the Day of Resurrection, nor will He purify them, and there is a painful punishment for them." [208]

كَلَّا إِنَّهُم عَن رَبِّهِم يَومَئِذٍ لَمَحجوبونَ

"No indeed! They will be veiled from their Lord on that day." [209]

---

[207] Nasr, H. (2015). *The Study Quran.* New York: Harper Collins
[208] Qurān 3:77
[209] Qurān 83:15

If God's punishment to the transgressors, is manifested through not speaking to them, not looking at them, and veiling them from Himself, it can be understood that His reward to the righteous, would conversely be the opposite. God will reward His righteous servants with His loving attention, speak to them with fondness, and remove any veils that may bar them from witnessing His Grandeur.

Whatever Their Souls Desire

Every human being has certain aspirations and desires, some of which are attainable and achievable, while others exist outside the realm of possibility. Even as a guest of the most gracious of hosts, the amenities and comforts made available, are naturally limited. This reality is one of the stark differences between this earthly life and the paradisal experience. In Paradise, the believers are granted whatever their souls desire, without even the need of verbalizing their wishes. These desires encompass both the physical and the spiritual. In one verse, God declares,

وَالَّذِينَ آمَنُوا وَعَمِلُوا الصّالِحاتِ فِي رَوضاتِ الجَنّاتِ ۖ لَهُم ما يَشاءونَ عِندَ رَبِّهِم ۚ ذلِكَ هُوَ الفَضلُ الكَبِيرُ

"...but those who have faith and do righteous deeds will be in the gardens of Paradise: they will have whatever they wish near their Lord. That is the greatest grace." [210]

Some commentators have interpreted the expression, "near their Lord" alongside the phrase, "that is the greatest grace",

---

[210] Qurān 42:22

126

as a reference to the spiritual delights. In another verse, the Qurān asserts this idea of unrestricted pleasures when it says,

لَهُم مَا يَشَاءونَ عِندَ رَبِّهِم ۚ ذَلِكَ جَزَاءُ المُحسِنِينَ

"They will have whatever they wish near their Lord. That is the reward of the virtuous." [211]

This verse, along with many others, highlight the limitless material and spiritual bounties at the disposal of the righteous in Paradise. In the earthly world, human beings are often barred from achieving what they desire because of restrictive forces within themselves, and unfavorable external conditions. Unlike the temporal world, no such impediments exist in Paradise. God, through his infinite grace and generosity, will bestow upon the denizens of Paradise, the ability to bring something into existence by merely desiring it.

Remarkably, the Qurān takes it a step further, and asserts that the inhabitants of Paradise will be granted rewards that exceed their wishes and desires. God offers this extraordinary glad tiding when He says,

لَهُم مَا يَشَاءونَ فِيها وَلَدَينا مَزِيدٌ

"There they will have whatever they wish, and with Us there is yet more." [212]

Some commentators interpret the expression "and with Us there is yet more", as a reference to the vision of God experienced by the heart. The rapturous joy of witnessing God

---

[211] Qurān 39:34
[212] Qurān 50:35

127

is believed to be the greatest blessing, beyond all else, that one can desire in Paradise. The great Persian poet, Rumi, once said, "I once had a thousand desires, but in my one desire to know you, all else melted away."

Unfathomable Bounties

Like the incomprehensible material blessings, the spiritual rewards that await God's servants are unfathomable. The descriptive accounts of the mystical pleasures, can never do justice to the actual experience. The following verse underscores this notion:

فَلا تَعلَمُ نَفسٌ ما أُخفِيَ لَهُم مِن قُرَّةِ أَعيُنٍ جَزاءً بِما كانوا يَعمَلونَ

"No one knows what has been kept hidden for them of comfort as a reward for what they used to do." [213]

One of the Prophet's Companions, Mu'ādth ibn Jabal, reported that the Prophet cited this verse when teaching him the practice of Islam:

يارسول الله، أنبئني بعمل يدخلني الجنّة، ويباعدني من النار، قال: "لقد سألت عن عظيم وإنّه ليسير على من يسّره الله عليه: تعبد الله ولا تشرك به شيئاً، وتقيم الصلاة المكتوبة، وتؤدّي الزكاة المفروضة، وتصوم شهر رمضان

قال: "وإن شئت أنبأتك بأبواب الخير" قال: قلت: أجل يارسول الله، قال: "الصوم جنّة، والصدقة تكفّر الخطيئة، وقيام الرجل في جوف الليل يبتغي وجه الله" ثمّ قرأ هذه الآية

---

[213] Qurān 32:17

"I said, 'O Messenger of God, tell me an act that will take me into the Garden and will keep me away from the Fire.' He replied, 'You have asked me about a significant matter; yet it is easy for him whom God Almighty makes it easy. You should worship God, associate nothing with Him, perform prayers, pay alms, fast during Ramadan, and make the pilgrimage to the House.' Then he said, 'Shall I not show you the gates of goodness? Fasting which is a shield; charity, which extinguishes sin as water extinguishes fire; and the prayer of a man in the depths of night'. Then the Prophet recited Surat al-Sajdah, verse 17. [214]

In a well-known tradition, it is reported that God once revealed to the Holy Prophet, that He has prepared unfathomable delights for the believers. The Holy Prophet once said,

ان الله يقول اعددت لعبادي الصالحين مالا عين رات ولا اذن سمعت ولا خطر على قلب بشر

"Verily, God says, 'I have prepared for My righteous servants what no eye has ever seen, and no ear has ever heard and no human heart has ever imagined'." [215]

Eternal Bliss

Human beings are predisposed to crave the infinite. If man was given a valley of gold, he would set out in search of more. Deep within every individual, is a desire for immortality, which is precisely why so many people fear death.

---

[214] Majma' al- Bayān, see Sūrah 32 verse 17
[215] Sahīh Bukhārī, v. 9, hadīth 589

They perceive death as the end of their existence. One of the distinguishing features of Paradise is its eternal nature. Contrary to the earthly world, which is the abode of temporality and mortality, Paradise has no end nor will its inhabitants ever perish. Its bounties are everlasting and its enjoyments are ceaseless.

In Paradise, the craving for the eternal and infinite will finally be quenched. The looming cloud of death and mortality, will no longer hover over their heads. In comparing this worldly life with the hereafter, the Qurān sheds light on two important distinctions:

بَل تُؤثِرونَ الحَياةَ الدُنيا وَالآخِرَةُ خَيرٌ وأبقى

"Rather you prefer the life of this world, while the Hereafter is better and more lasting." [216]

In this verse, Paradise is described as being "better" and "more lasting" in comparison to life in this world. In the earthly life, human beings experience both pain and pleasure. They endure sickness and cope with loss. Not a single day passes without some form of discomfort afflicting even the most affluent of people. Put simply, pain is an inevitable aspect of the human condition. Paradise, on the other hand, is better because it offers a pain free existence. It is a life of pleasure and no pain.

It is "more lasting" because its enjoyments never end, and its residents are never asked to leave. The denizens of Paradise will enjoy the bounties of their Lord with the comfort of knowing that they are in their eternal home in the presence of the Lord of the Worlds.

---

[216] Qurān 87:16-17

Chapter Five: The Gates, Vastness and Stations of Paradise

The Gates

Every home, building or garden is typically designed with a point of entry in the form of a door or a gate. Similarly, the believers are said to enter Paradise through its official entrances known as 'the Gates of Paradise'. Gates are normally designed with locks and keys, but these gates have metaphorical keys that grant access to different classes of believers. The metaphorical keys are references to certain noble actions that were performed by these individuals in their earthly lives. The Holy Qurān makes mention of these gates in several verses, and asserts that Paradise anxiously awaits the arrival of the righteous with its gates opened wide. God Almighty says,

وَسِيقَ الَّذِينَ اتَّقَوْا رَبَّهُم إِلَى الجَنَّةِ زُمَرًا ۖ حَتَّى إِذَا جَاءُوهَا وَفُتِحَتْ أَبْوَابُهَا وَقَالَ لَهُم خَزَنَتُهَا سَلَامٌ عَلَيْكُم طِبْتُم فَادْخُلُوهَا خَالِدِينَ

"Those who are conscious of their Lord will be led to Paradise in throngs. When they reach it, and its gates are opened, its keepers will say to them, 'Peace be to you! You are welcome! Enter it to remain [forever]'." [217]

When the believers are escorted to the gates of Paradise, they will not be required to knock or exert any effort to open its gates, because the gates will open upon their arrival. It is as though Paradise is impatiently awaiting the coming of its honorable residents. In another verse, the Qurān asserts,

جَنَّاتِ عَدْنٍ مُفَتَّحَةً لَهُمُ الأبوابُ

"...the Gardens of Eden, whose gates are flung open for them." [218]

The word مُفَتَّحَةً, according to Arabic syntax, follows the pattern of تفعيل, and in this context, implies multiplicity and emphasis. In other words, all the gates, not just one, are flung open for the believers. They are not simply unlocked or even opened slightly, they are opened wide to welcome the righteous servants of God.

Do the gates of Paradise open on their own as though they possess an independent consciousness? Or do they open because of the spiritual energy of the believers when they approach? Do the gates open in response to the will and desire of the righteous? Or is it the angels who open its gates and at the entrances to greet the throngs of believers? It is difficult to draw a definitive conclusion from the Qurānic verses, because the act of opening the gate is not explicitly attributed

---

[217] Qurān 39:73
[218] Qurān 38:50

134

to anyone. Many scholars however, subscribe to the view that the gates of Paradise possess a degree of consciousness and open wide to receive the pious.

Upon entering Paradise and settling into their new home, the believers are greeted by the angels. In the following verse, the Qurān makes mention of this grand welcoming:

وَالمَلائِكَةُ يَدخُلونَ عَلَيهِم مِن كُلِّ بابٍ سَلامٌ عَلَيكُم بِما صَبَرتُمْ ۚ فَنِعمَ عُقبَى الدّارِ

"...and the angels will enter upon them from every door: 'Peace be to you, for your patience.' How excellent is the reward of the [ultimate] abode!" [219]

Both Paradise and Hell have gates. The number of Hell's gates is explicitly mentioned in the Holy Qurān in the following verse:

لَها سَبعَةُ أبوابٍ

"It has seven gates..." [220]

The Holy Qurān indicates that Paradise has multiple gates, due to its usage of the plural form of gate أبوابٌ. However, no verse specifies the exact number of gates. A perusal of hadīth literature reveals the existence of eight gates leading into the paradisal garden. Hellfire has seven gates while Paradise has eight. This seems to suggest that the paths leading to Paradise are more than the roads leading to Hell.

In a well-known tradition, Imam Alī (a.s.) speaks of the eight gates of Paradise when he says,

---

[219] Qurān 13:23-24
[220] Qurān 15:44

إنَّ لِلجَنَّةِ ثَمانِيَةَ أبواب: بابٌ يَدخُلُ مِنهُ النَّبِيُّونَ والصِّدِّيقُونَ، وبابٌ يَدخُلُ مِنهُ الشُّهَداءُ والصّالِحُونَ، وخَمسَةُ أبْوابٍ يَدخُلُ مِنها شِيعَتُنا ومُحِبّونا ...، وبابٌ يَدخُلُ مِنهُ سائِرُ المُسلِمِينَ مِمَّنْ شَهِدَ أنْ لا إلهَ إلّا اللهُ، ولَم يَكُنْ فِي قَلبِهِ مِقْدارُ ذَرَّةٍ مِنْ بُغْضِنا أهلَ البَيتِ.

"Paradise has eight gates: a gate through which the prophets and the truthful ones will enter, a gate through which the martyrs and the righteous will enter, five gates through which our followers and our lovers will enter ..., a gate through which the rest of the Muslims will enter, that is, those that bear witness to 'There is no god but god' and who do not bear an atom's weight of enmity towards us, the Ahlul Bayt." [221]

للجنة ثمانية أبواب..... فمن كان من أهل الصلاة دُعي من باب الصلاة ومن كان من أهل الصيام دعي من باب الريان ومن كان من أهل الصدقة دعي من باب الصدقة ومن كان من أهل الجهاد دُعي من باب الجهاد

According to another hadīth we similarly find, "Paradise has eight gates. [Four are:] Whosoever was among the people of prayer shall be called from the gate of prayer. Whosoever was among the people of fasting shall be called from the gate of fasting. Whosoever was among the people of charity shall be called from the gate of charity. Whosoever was among the people of striving shall be called from the gate of striving." [222]

In a tradition from Imam Muhammad al- Bāqir (a.s.), the vastness of each gate is described:

[221] al-Khisāl, p. 408, no. 6
[222] Bukhārī, hadīth 1897

احسنوا الظن بالله واعلموا ان للجنة ثمانية ابواب , عرض كل منها مسيرة اربعين سنة

"Have a good opinion of God and know that Paradise has eight gates. The width of each gate is [equivalent to] forty years of travel." [223]

There are also other narrations that assert that the gates of Paradise, signify certain holy personalities, whereby through their emulation, people will be granted entrance into the gardens of bliss. It is reported that Imam Mūsa al-Kādhim (a.s.) once said,

ان عليا باب من ابواب الجنة

"Indeed Alī is a gate from among the gates of Paradise." [224]

In addition to the numbers and names of the gates of Paradise, traditions also speak of inscriptions on the gates of Paradise. These inscriptions encapsulate some of the paramount virtues that allow people to be admitted into the paradisal garden. They essentially represent the great ideals and moral principles enshrined by the Qurān and the legacy of the Holy Prophet (s.a) and his immaculate family.

It is reported from Jābir ibn Abdillah al-Ansārī, that the Holy Prophet said,

مكتوب على باب الجنة لا اله الا الله محمد رسول الله , علي اخو رسول الله

---

[223] Bihār al-Anwār, v. 8, p. 121
[224] al-Kāfī, v. 2, p. 389

137

"It is written on the gate of Paradise 'There is no god but God, Muhammad is the Messenger of God, Alī is the brother of God's Messenger'."[225]

In a lengthy narration detailing the Prophet's heavenly ascension, the Holy Prophet (s.a.) recalls the inscriptions he saw on the various gates of Paradise:

لما أسرى بي إلى السماء قال لي جبرئيل: قد أمرت الجنة والنار أن تعرض عليك، قال: فرأيت الجنة وما فيها من النعيم، ورأيت النار وما فيها من العذاب، والجنة فيها ثمانية أبواب، على كل باب منها أربع كلمات، كل كلمة خير من الدنيا وما فيها لمن يعلم ويعمل بها، وللنار سبعة أبواب، على كل باب منها ثلاث كلمات، كل كلمة خير من الدنيا وما فيها لمن يعلم ويعمل بها

"When I was led in ascension into heaven, Gabriel (a.s.) said to me, 'Paradise and Hell have been commanded to come before you'. He Prophet (s.a.) said, 'I saw Paradise and what it contains from blessings and I saw Hell and what it consists from torment. Paradise has eight gates. On each gate, there are four words. Each word is worth more than this world and what is therein, only for those who appreciate (their meaning) and put them into practice. While Hell has seven gates, on each gate there are 3 words. Each word is worth more than this world and what is therein, only for those who appreciate (their meaning) and put them into practice'."

قال لي جبرئيل: اقرأ يا محمد ما على الابواب فقرأت ذلك

"Gabriel said to me, 'O Muhammad read what is written on the gates', I thus read."

---

[225] Bihār al-Anwār, v. 8, p. 131

أما أبواب الجنة فعلى أول باب منها مكتوب: لا إله إلا الله، محمد رسول الله،
علي ولي الله، لكل شيء حلية وحيلة العيش أربع خصال: القناعة، وبذل الحق،
وترك الحقد، ومجالسة أهل الخير.

"As for the gates of Paradise, it is written on the first of its gates: There is no god but God. Muhammad is the messenger of God. Alī is the friend of God. For everything there is a key, and life's key consists of four qualities: To have contentment, to sacrifice for the truth, to refrain from malice and to be in the company of virtuous people."

وعلى الباب الثاني مكتوب: لا إله إلا الله، محمد رسول الله، علي ولي الله، لكل
شيء حيلة وحيلة السرور في الآخرة أربع خصال: مسح رؤوس اليتامى،
والتعطف على الارامل، والسعي في حوائج المؤمنين، والتفقد للفقراء
والمساكين.

"On the second gate, it is written: There is no god but God. Muhammad is the messenger of God. Alī is the friend of God'. For everything there is a key, and the key for happiness consists of four qualities: To wipe over the head of orphans, to show affection towards the widows, to strive in fulfilling the needs of believers, and to check on the poor and the needy."

وعلى الباب الثالث مكتوب: لا إله إلا الله، محمد رسول الله، علي ولي الله، لكل
شئ حيلة وحيلة الصحة في الدنيا أربع خصال: قلة الكلام، وقلة المنام، وقلة
المشي، وقلة الطعام.

"On the third gate it is written: There is no god but God. Muhammad is the messenger of God. Alī is the friend of God. For everything there is a key, and the key for good health in this world consists of four qualities: to speak little, sleep little, walk little and eat little."

على الباب الرابع مكتوب: لا إله إلا الله، محمد رسول الله، علي ولي الله، من كان يؤمن بالله واليوم الآخر فليكرم ضيفه من كان يؤمن بالله واليوم الآخر فليكرم جاره، من كان يؤمن بالله واليوم الآخر فليكرم والديه، من كان يؤمن بالله واليوم الآخر فليقل خيرا أو يسكت

"On the fourth gate it is written: There is no god but God. Muhammad is the messenger of God. Alī is the friend of God. Let him who believes in God and the Last Day be hospitable towards his guest. Let him who believes in God and the Last Day, be generous towards his neighbor. Let him who believes in God and the last Day, be kind towards his parents. Let him who believes in God and the Last Day, either speak good or remain silent."

وعلى الباب الخامس مكتوب: لا إله إلا الله، محمد رسول الله، علي ولي الله، من أراد أن لا يظلم فلا يظلم، ومن أراد أن لا يشتم فلا يشتم، ومن أراد أن لا يذل فلا يذل، ومن أراد أن يستمسك بالعروة الوثقى في الدنيا والآخرة فليقل: لا إله إلا الله، محمد رسول الله، علي ولي الله

"On the fifth gate it is written: There is no god but God. Muhammad is the messenger of God. Alī is the friend of God. Let him who does not want to be oppressed, not oppress others. Let him who does not wish to be slandered, not slander others.

Let him who does not want to be humiliated, not humiliate others and let him who wishes to hold fast to the most trustworthy handhold that never breaks, in this world and the Hereafter, say: There is no god but God. Muhammad is the messenger of God. Alī is the friend of God."

وعلى الباب السادس مكتوب: لا إله إلا الله، محمد رسول الله، علي ولي الله، من أراد أن يكون قبره وسيعا فسيحا فليبن المساجد، ومن أراد أن لا تأكله الديدان تحت الارض فليسكن المساجد ومن أحب أن يكون طريا مطرا لا يبلى فليكنس المساجد ومن أحب أن يرى موضعه في الجنة فليكس المساجد بالبسط.

"On the sixth gate it is written: There is no god but God. Muhammad is the messenger of God. Alī is the friend of God. Let him who wishes to have his grave wide and broad, build mosques. Let him who does not wish to be eaten by earth worms attend the mosques. Let him who wants his body to remain soft, tender and never be decomposed, sweep the (floors) of the mosques and let him who wants to witness his place in Paradise, cover the (floors) of mosques with rugs."

وعلى الباب السابع مكتوب: لا إله إلا الله، محمد رسول الله، علي ولي الله، بياض القلب في أربع خصال: عيادة المريض، واتباع الجنائز، وشراء الاكفان، ورد القرض.

"On the seventh gate it is written: There is no god but God. Muhammad is the messenger of God. Alī is the friend of God. The purity of the heart is found in four qualities: In visiting the sick, participating in funerals, in purchasing shrouds and repaying loans."

وعلى الباب الثامن مكتوب: لا إله إلا الله، محمد رسول الله، علي ولي الله، من أراد الدخول من هذه الابواب فليتمسك بأربع خصال: السخاء، وحسن الخلق، والصدقة، والكف عن أذى عباد الله تعالى.

"On the eighth gate it is written: There is no god but God. Muhammad is the messenger of God. Alī is the friend of God: Let him who wishes to enter from these gates, hold fast to four qualities: generosity, good manners, charity and abstention from harming the servants of God." [226]

The Vastness

The earthly life that human beings occupy, is undoubtedly much more limited and restricted in comparison to the sheer expansiveness of the hereafter. The human being began his journey in this earthly realm as a fetus in the womb of his mother. God brought him into being, and meticulously fashioned him. The fetus knows nothing other than the small womb he or she occupies. Upon completion of a full-term pregnancy, the fetus transitions from the dark, narrow womb into the vast and exceedingly spacious world. After tarrying in this earthly world, death triggers a new birth into a tremendously vaster world known as the hereafter. With death, the human being leaves the metaphorical womb of this world, and enters a world that is unfathomably immense. Of the vastness of Paradise, the Qurān asserts,

---

[226] Bihār al-Anwār, v. 8, p. 145

سَابِقُوا إِلَىٰ مَغْفِرَةٍ مِن رَّبِّكُم وَجَنَّةٍ عَرْضُهَا كَعَرْضِ السَّمَاءِ وَالأَرْضِ أُعِدَّت لِلَّذِينَ آمَنُوا بِاللَّهِ وَرُسُلِهِ

"Hasten towards forgiveness from your Lord and a Paradise as vast as the heavens and the earth, prepared for those who have faith in God and His messengers..." [227]

وَسَارِعُوا إِلَىٰ مَغْفِرَةٍ مِن رَّبِّكُم وَجَنَّةٍ عَرْضُهَا السَّمَاوَاتُ وَالأَرْضُ أُعِدَّت لِلْمُتَّقِينَ

"And hasten towards your Lord's forgiveness and a Paradise as vast as the heavens and the earth, prepared for the pious." [228]

In order to appreciate the message of this verse, it is important to shed some light on the vastness of the universe. The verse explicitly compares the vastness of Paradise to the vastness of the universe. The question that naturally arises is, "how big is the universe"? Astrophysicists speculate that there are over 100 billion galaxies in the universe.[229] Each galaxy containing billions of stars like our sun and even larger.[230] Scientists estimate that there are more stars in the universe than grains of sand on earth.[231] It is virtually impossible to accurately determine the size of the universe due to its continual expansion but recently cosmologists have asserted that the observable universe at the present moment is approximately 92 billion light-years in diameter.[232] That means it would take light, which travels at a rapid speed of 186,000 miles per second, 92 billion years to travel from one side of the universe

---

[227] Qurān 57:21

[228] Qurān 3:133

[229] Ryden, B. (2016). *Introduction to cosmology*. New York: Cambridge University Press

[230] Ibid.

[231] Ibid.

[232] Ibid.

to the other side.[233]

Of the immense scale of the universe, Dr. Luke Davies, a British physicist, says,

> The whole universe is littered with galaxies just like the Milky Way and Andromeda, and using our most powerful telescopes we can see light from galaxies that has taken more than 13 billion years to reach us... The universe is about 13.8 billion years old, so any light we see has to have been travelling for 13.8 billion years or less – we call this the 'observable universe'. However, the distance to the edge of the observable universe is about 46 billion light years because the universe is expanding all the time.... So how big is our universe? Well we don't really know, but it's big. So big that even light hasn't had time to cross it in nearly 14 billion years! And it's still getting bigger all of the time.[234]

In another verse, the Qurān describes the vastness of Paradise as a "great kingdom". God Almighty says,

وَإِذَا رَأَيْتَ ثَمَّ رَأَيْتَ نَعِيمًا وَمُلْكًا كَبِيرًا

"As you look, you will see there bliss and a great kingdom."[235]

Many interpretations have been put forward regarding the meaning of the expression, "a great kingdom". Some maintain that it refers to the sheer immensity of Paradise. One narration captures the enormity of that kingdom when it says:

---

[233] Ibid.
[234] Davies, L. (2015), 'How big is the universe?'. Science Network.
[235] Qurān 76:20

ان ادناهم منزلة ينظر في ملكه من مسيرة الف عام

"Verily, the lowest of them in rank will look upon his kingdom from the distance of one thousand years." [236]

The kingdom given to the lowest ranking believer will be such that his palaces, servants, and gardens will extend beyond the range of his sight. It would take one thousand years of travel to explore the paradisal property given to a single believer occupying the lowest station. Other traditions put the number at two thousand. Putting aside these minor discrepancies, it is unequivocally clear that, like the incomprehensible blessings of Paradise, the size of Paradise stands equally inscrutable.

The Stations

Divine justice dictates, that equal reward cannot be granted to believers of varying degrees of faith and moral excellence. The recompense of one who was steadfast, and made noble sacrifices, cannot be equated with one who settled for spiritual mediocrity. The Holy Qurān asserts that on the Day of Resurrection, the believers will be divided into two main groups, namely the companions of the right hand and the foremost:

وَكُنتُم أَزواجًا ثَلاثَةً فَأَصحابُ المَيمَنَةِ ما أَصحابُ المَيمَنَةِ وَأَصحابُ المَشأَمَةِ ما أَصحابُ المَشأَمَةِ وَالسّابِقونَ السّابِقونَ أُولئِكَ المُقَرَّبونَ

---

[236] Tafsīr Majma' al-Bayān, v. 9, p. 411

"...you will be three groups: The Companions of the Right Hand—and what are the Companions of the Right Hand? And the Companions of the Left Hand—and what are the Companions of the Left Hand? And the Foremost Ones are the foremost ones. They are the ones brought near [to God]." [237]

Within the two groups there are subgroups, each constituting people of varying spiritual rank. In the following tradition from the Holy Prophet (s.a.), the difference in reward between the average believers and the spiritual elite is highlighted:

جنتان من ذهب للمقربين , وجنتان من ورق لاصحاب اليمين

"Two gardens of gold for the ones brought near [to God], and two gardens of silver, for the companions of the right hand." [238]

The usage of gold and silver in this narration, is interpreted as a reference to the difference in quality between the gardens. Those occupying the higher stations of Paradise, enjoy luxuries and comforts that are unavailable to the residents of lower levels.

As discussed in chapter two, the word جنة literally means "garden", and is typically used to describe Paradise. Some verses employ its singular form (جنة) while others use its plural form جنات. If examined in isolation, the verses that speak of a single garden, may lead one to mistakenly assume that Paradise is an egalitarian utopia. One such verse is the following:

---

[237] Qurān 56:7-11
[238] Tafsīr al-Dur al-Manthūr, v. 6, p. 146

قُل أَذٰلِكَ خَيْرٌ أَم جَنَّةُ الخُلْدِ الَّتِي وُعِدَ المُتَّقُونَ ۚ كَانَت لَهُم جَزَاءً وَمَصِيرًا

"Say, 'Is that better, or the everlasting Paradise promised to the pious, which will be their reward and destination?'".[239]

Although the singular form for Paradise is used, it in no way negates the existence of degrees and levels within Paradise. The verse simply assigns a general adjective to Paradise, describing it as being "everlasting". The eternal nature of Paradise applies to the highest stations, as well as the lowest stations.

There are numerous verses throughout the Qurān, that explicitly make mention of multiple gardens. God has prepared copious gardens for the believers as the following verse conveys:

أُولَٰئِكَ لَهُم جَنَّاتُ عَدْنٍ تَجْرِي مِن تَحْتِهِمُ الأَنْهَارُ

"For such there will be the Gardens of Eden with rivers running in them."[240]

The term "Gardens of Eden" occurs eleven times in the Qurān. This repetition points to the significance of this description, and its implications. Some commentators have understood "the Gardens of Eden" to be an especially exalted or blessed place. Several possible meanings have been put forward which include:

1. The Gardens of Eden refer to the center of Paradise and the focal point of all its blessings.

---

[239] Qurān 25:15
[240] Qurān 18:31

2. The Gardens of Eden represent the highest echelons of Paradise reserved for the spiritual elite.
3. The Gardens of Eden denotes a special place in Paradise whose palace is the Divine Throne.
4. The Gardens of Eden signify the lavish palaces of gold which only the prophets, martyrs, and just rulers will reside.

Others see the word عَدْنٍ, Eden, not as the name of a place, but as an adjective modifying the word "gardens", meaning "gardens in which to dwell". Irrespective of the view that one finds most plausible, one can infer from the verse that within Paradise, there are places that are more exalted than others.

In one verse, the Holy Qurān makes mention of the highest level in Paradise. The existence of a highest level implies the existence of lower levels, and supports the notion of a stratified Paradise. The pinnacle of Paradise is described as الفِردَوسِ, Firdaws in the following verse:

إِنَّ الَّذِينَ آمَنوا وَعَمِلُوا الصّالِحاتِ كانَت لَهُم جَنّاتُ الفِردَوسِ نُزُلًا

"As for those who have faith and do righteous deeds they shall have the gardens of Firdaws as a welcome." [241]

It is reported that the Holy Prophet (s.a.) once encouraged his companions to ask God to grant them the Firdaws saying:

اذا سالتم الله تعالى فاسالوه الفردوس , فانه وسط الجنة واعلا الجنة وفوقه عرش الرحمن , ومنها تفجر انهارالجنة

Qurān 18:107

"If you ask God [for something] ask Him for the Firdaws for it is the center of Paradise, and the highest part of Paradise and above it, is the throne of the Beneficent, and from it gushes forth the rivers of Paradise". [242]

It is also narrated that Imam Alī ibn Abī Tālib (a.s.) spoke about the loftiness of the Firdaws, and those who will be its honorable occupants.

لكل شي ذروة وذروة الجنة الفردوس وهي لمحمد وآل محمد

"Everything has a highpoint and the highpoint of Paradise is the Firdaws and it belongs to Muhammad and the family of Muhammad." [243]

As mentioned earlier, the presence of a highpoint in Paradise, implies the existence of lower stations. A common misconception among many, is that Paradise is a generic, single-level abode, where God rewards all believers equally. Imam Alī(a.s.), in describing Paradise, once said,

دَرَجاتٌ مُتَفاضِلاتٌ، ومَنازِلُ مُتَفاوِتاتٌ

"There are degrees differing in excellence, and various stations". [244]

Imam al- Sādiq (a.s.), also dispels this fallacy in the following narration:

لاتقولن واحدة ان الله يقول : ومن دونهما جنتان , ولاتقولن درجة واحدة ان الله يقول : درجات بعضها فوق بعض , وانما تفاضل القوم بالاعمال

---

[242] Tafsīr Rūh al-Ma'āni, v. 16, p. 147
[243] Tafsīr al-Mīzān, see Sūrah18 verse 107
[244] Nahj al-Balāgha, Sermon 85

"Do not say one [garden] for verily God says: 'And beneath these two are two gardens.' And do not say [Paradise is] one degree for God says: 'Degrees one above the other'. Surely, the distinction of people is based on deeds." [245]

If the Holy Qurān and hadīth literature both assert the existence of varying degrees within Paradise, the question that naturally arises is, how many levels are there in Paradise? The answer to this question is revealed in a tradition reported from Imam Alī ibn al-Hussain (a.s.) wherein he says,

عَلَيكَ بالقُرآنِ، فإنَّ اللهَ خَلقَ الجَنَّـةَ ... وجَعَلَ دَرَجاتِها عَلى قَدْرِ آياتِ القُرآنِ، فمَن قَرأ القُرآنَ، قالَ لَهُ: إِقْرَأ وارْقَ، ومَن دَخَـلَ مِنهُمُ الجَنَّةَ لَم يَكُنْ فَي الجَنَّةِ أعْلى دَرَجَـةً مِنهُ ما خَلا النَّبِيِّينَ والصِّدِّيقينَ

"Adhere to the Qurān...for God has created Paradise, and has made its stations in accordance with the verses of the Qurān. So whoever reads the Qur'an, it will say to him, 'Read and ascend!' So whoever from among them enters Paradise, there will not be a station higher than theirs except for the prophets and the truthful ones." [246]

According to this narration, the degrees of Paradise are equivalent to the verses of the Holy Qurān which exceed 6000 verses. Thus, there are over 6000 different levels within Paradise. Even the lowest level of Paradise contains blessings that surpass anything experienced during one's earthly life. Imam al-Sādiq (a.s.) offers an astounding description of the lowest degree of Paradise in the following tradition:

إِنَّ أدنَى أَهلِ الجَنَّةِ مَنزِلاً لَو نَزَلَ بِهِ الثَّقَلانِ ـ الجِنُّ والإِنسُ ـ لَوَسِعَهُم طَعاماً وشَراباً، ولا يَنْقُصُ مِمَّا عِندَهُ شَيءٌ

---

[245] Tafsīr Majma' al-Bayān, v. 9, p. 210
[246] Bihār al-Anwār, v. 8, p.133

"For the one who occupies the lowest station in Paradise, were the humans and the jinn to appear as guests for him, nothing would diminish from him if he were to provide them all with food and drink." [247]

This book was intended to give the reader a glimpse into the wondrous world of Paradise. Praise be to God, who has shown his servants the many paths that lead to the gardens of bliss. Let us remain steadfast and strive to become the recipients of its material and spiritual gifts. May God inspire us with the ambition to attain its highest stations in the company of the Holy Prophet and his immaculate progeny.

---

[247] Bihār al-Anwār, v. 8, p. 120

Index

A

abuse 24

acceptance 28, 29, 35

action.............18, 19, 20, 27, 83

advantageous..........................36

adversaries.............................83

affection 102

affliction........................25, 26

affluent 96

agitation................................80

ailments 79

allergy 47

allurements............................37

amenities 49, 72, 93

amenity..................................55

amusements...........................89

angels 15, 30, 72, 75, 76, 77, 85, 99

animals 32, 33, 58

anxiety.................20, 47, 80, 81

ascension 11, 12, 14, 101, 102

atonement..............................31

attachment............22, 23, 37, 38

attributes...............32, 60, 68, 74

audience 30

aura.......................................79

authenticity...........................83

B

balance 53

bathing...................................31

battle....................................35

beauty.......54, 59, 66, 69, 70, 71

bed...54

belief 11, 15, 18, 19, 35, 57

birds.....................................33

blemishes.........................57, 79

blessings....7, 23, 43, 73, 74, 76, 80, 81, 87, 94, 102, 107, 109, 111

blind 22, 39

blood 47

bond......................................35

bounties 23, 73, 77, 94, 96

bracelets 66, 67

branches 44, 45, 46, 48

breezes..................................49

brocade......................51, 52, 65

C

calmative 60

calmness.........................49, 86

camphor...........................60, 61

canopied 53

carnivorous............................57

carpets 54

certainty...............................21

chaos 47

charity ...33, 37, 38, 50, 95, 100, 104

chastity 70

cheerfulness...........................87

circumambulating 71

civilization.............................24

civilizations...........................66

cleanliness 47

cleanse..................................40

color 31, 34, 47, 65

comfort 8, 48, 50, 54, 55, 71, 86, 95, 96

comforts 8, 54, 93, 108

community 24, 77

composure 51, 86

conceal 44, 87

consciousness.............15, 20, 99

construction...........................14

consumption..13, 29, 43, 55, 57, 59

contamination.........................61

contentment...78, 84, 85, 89, 90, 102

contraction.............................48

conviction..............................21

coral......................................69

corruption..............................22

creed.....................................34

culinary 64

cushions............................51, 54

D

dangerous 37, 39, 80

Date-palms 56

daughter............................13, 14

deaf.......................................39

death...............7, 79, 83, 96, 105

debased..................................77

deceit.....................................84

defeat.....................................83

deficiencies 76

delicacy 61

density 46

deserts 45

desires20, 22, 23, 68, 73, 78, 93, 94

destruction..................12, 15, 33

detestable...............................40

detriment 36, 37

devious 85

devotion......................24, 26, 71

diet..57

difficulty................................26

dignity 34, 65

discomfort 47, 48, 96

disobedience...............20, 26, 28

disregard.................................92

distinction24, 40, 53, 56, 69, 70, 75, 111

disturbance 50, 80

Divine favors............................7

drinks..........8, 58, 60, 61, 62, 64

dumb 39

duties 20, 39

E

eat...............................33, 103

economic 18

elevation...............................49

elite.................24, 29, 108, 109

elongation............................48

emotional.........................50, 80

emotions......................55, 80, 88

emulation............................101

energy........................50, 54, 99

enlivened 59

enmity 78, 80, 100

entrée.....................................55

envy.......................................84

eternal life 7

ethical....................................18

everlasting.....48, 54, 77, 87, 96, 108, 109

excellence.................21, 71, 107

exemplars 35

exotic.............................45, 46

expansion 14, 106

expensive...............................65

eyes 44, 46, 63, 69, 73, 91, 92

F

fabric 51, 54, 65

faith 7, 11, 15, 18, 19, 21, 24, 28, 34, 35, 36, 38, 46, 50, 81, 91, 93, 105, 107, 110

falsehood.........................35, 84

fasting............................36, 100

faults.....................................76

fear 11, 20, 22, 23, 25, 38, 47, 80, 81, 83, 96

fetus...............................44, 105

fierce 24

Firdaws.......................109, 110

folklore..................................54

food ...14, 29, 55, 56, 57, 58, 64, 72, 90, 112

forbearance............................20

forest 14

forgetfulness..........................20

foundational 70

fragile 30

fragrance 13

freshness....................46, 65, 87

friend........32, 35, 102, 103, 104

friends 35, 81, 82

fruit.....13, 18, 33, 46, 55, 56, 57

funerals...............................104

furnishings........................8, 51

G

Gabriel....................12, 13, 102

gardens 8, 17, 24, 28, 36, 44, 45, 46, 56, 58, 69, 70, 76, 80, 89, 93, 101, 107, 108, 109, 110, 111, 112

garments 8, 25, 43, 65, 66, 90

Gates 8, 97, 98

gaze 70, 92

generosity 94, 104

generous 11, 26, 103

ginger 60, 61

glances.....................................70

gold ...15, 23, 46, 52, 53, 64, 66, 67, 96, 108, 109

grandeur 67, 74

grave...............................22, 104

graves 92

graveyard.................................58

greed.......................................38

greenery...................................45

grief......................28, 80, 81, 82

grievance 83

guardian...........................13, 78

guest 93, 103

guests........................51, 72, 112

H

happiness 23, 78, 84, 86, 87, 102

hardship................26, 77, 79, 81

health..............................26, 103

heedlessness 30

honesty 36

honey 58, 59

hospitable 103

hospitality...............................72

hostility 24, 50, 78

humiliate 103

humility 30

humorless 85

I

Imam Zaynul Abideen 8

immaterial 43, 76

impassioned............................77

impediments 94

imperfections..........................79

impurities 27, 59

Inanimate creatures 32

inception..................................78

indifference 92

indulgences 7, 74

injury......................................80

innovation 59

insane 44

inscriptions...........................101

instruments 39

integrity 36

interconnection.......................22

invigorated 59

invitation 20, 30

Irrational creatures 32

J

Jesus Christ 13
jinn 54, 70, 112
joke.................................85, 86
joy .8, 20, 54, 58, 63, 73, 78, 86, 87, 90, 94

K

keys 34, 98
Kingship...............................67
knowledge............20, 32, 59, 63

L

leaves...............................46, 105
lethal....................................30
loan......................................26
loans 104
locks 98
Lote Tree..............................12
lovable.................................85
love4, 22, 23, 27, 32, 34, 35, 37, 59, 60, 77, 81, 83, 86, 88, 90
luxuries....................46, 67, 108
luxurious 65
luxury 67

M

maidens 8, 68, 69, 70, 71
malice..................................102
malicious 24
martyrs 82, 83, 100, 109
mates 50, 53, 65

mattresses 51, 52
meat....................51, 55, 57, 58
medicine....................55, 61, 86
medicines 39
merit....................................24
metaphorical..15, 32, 38, 63, 98, 105
milk...............................58, 59
mirror 40, 87
misconception 85, 110
misfortune 79, 81
modesty 70
moon 25, 71, 77
mosques...............................104
mother 13, 44, 105
Mount Hira............................12
mu'min.................................21
musk...............................61, 62
mystical 94
mythical................................54

N

needy 102
negligence 20, 28, 39
nobility 40, 65, 71
noble..17, 21, 26, 29, 34, 40, 62, 63, 70, 72, 81, 83, 98, 107
nourish.................................55
nourishment...22, 28, 29, 46, 57, 59

O

Obedience 19

obedient..............................83

obscenity 86

obscurity.............................28

obsession 37

ointments............................39

opponents 35

oppress 103

opulent..................8, 54, 65, 66

orchards..............................44

orientalists...........................45

orphans 102

P

pain....26, 28, 29, 43, 79, 81, 88, 96

palace 46, 109

palaces.....................8, 107, 109

pampered............................71

Pardoning 40

parents 34, 103

passions 22, 23

Patience..........25, 26, 49, 77, 99

peace ...8, 35, 47, 49, 50, 51, 52, 78, 79, 80, 85, 86

pearls.........................53, 69, 71

peripheral 92

perish.............................78, 96

perpetual.........................14, 54

perseverance.........................24

personal 14, 18

Pharaoh 24, 35

philosophers 15

physician 39, 55

pilgrimage 95

pillows................................54

pious..10, 11, 24, 31, 60, 71, 77, 80, 81, 82, 99, 105, 108

plant...........................14, 29, 33

playful 85, 86

polytheism...........................27

pomegranates 56

poor 102

possessions 26

prayers 24, 29, 30, 31, 36, 37, 95

pregnancy 105

principles............21, 24, 64, 101

profound.........................21, 31

Prophet Zackariah 13

prosperity 17, 23, 51, 73, 79

protection 48, 49, 65, 80

provisions 13, 14

proximity...........................8, 63

punishment....11, 30, 33, 43, 92, 93

Q

Quraysh 14

R

rainfall................................14

Rational 32

raw materials 14, 15

rebellion 22, 23

recipient 38

reciprocate 40, 92

reckoning 13, 24

recompense 11, 36, 107

redemption 18

relaxation 48, 52

religiosity 19

remorse 28, 29

repairing 40

repentance 24, 27, 28, 29

resilience 24

resistance 40

resolution 28, 29

resting place 74

restrain 70

resurrection 43, 87

reward ... 7, 8, 10, 21, 36, 38, 43, 68, 72, 77, 87, 89, 93, 94, 95, 99, 107, 108

rhetoric 85

righteous 8, 18, 19, 21, 34, 35, 38, 58, 60, 70, 73, 76, 77, 81, 82, 83, 84, 93, 94, 95, 98, 99, 100, 110

righteousness 15, 18

ritual 29, 30, 37, 68

rivers ... 8, 44, 45, 46, 58, 59, 80, 109

role models 35

royalty 64, 67

rubies 53, 69

rug 51, 54

rugs 54, 55, 104

S

sacrifice 83, 102

safety 47, 80

salvation 17, 18, 30, 36, 87

scarce 56

scholars ... 11, 15, 21, 48, 73, 87, 89, 92, 99

Scientists 47, 106

security 47, 48, 49, 80

seeds 23

self-refinement 17

servants 8, 19, 24, 29, 34, 60, 61, 62, 71, 73, 81, 82, 83, 84, 90, 93, 94, 95, 99, 104, 107, 112

service 27, 71, 89

shelter 48

shining 77, 87

shortcomings 20

shrouds 104

sick 104

sickness 47, 96

sicknesses 79

silent 25, 103

silk 25, 43, 51, 52, 65

silver 15, 23, 64, 65, 67, 108

slander 103

sleep 103

social 8, 18, 53, 65, 66, 67, 84

social interactions...............8, 84

sofa...................................53, 54

speak ...36, 81, 92, 93, 101, 103, 108

speech.............20, 36, 84, 85, 90

spice 61

spiritual8, 18, 21, 22, 25, 29, 30, 31, 37, 39, 43, 50, 59, 60, 67, 70, 74, 75, 76, 87, 89, 91, 93, 94, 99, 107, 109, 112

splendor.....................46, 67, 87

spouse..............................53, 67

spouses 50, 53, 65, 67, 68, 87

spring..............60, 61, 62, 63, 86

springs 8

stability...................................47

star...77

stars 32, 71, 106

Stations..8, 9, 17, 45, 56, 59, 69, 70, 97, 107, 108, 109, 110, 111, 112

status-quo 24

steadfast......................107, 112

suffering 25, 26, 30

summer...................................14

sunlight.............................14, 48

supporters...............................35

supreme................55, 62, 77, 88

sustenance 29

symbolic................................92

system 18, 80

T

taqwa......................................20

temperature 48

thorns....................................56

throne 52, 54

torment 43, 102

tranquil 86, 90

tranquility.............43, 49, 50, 79

travel 47, 48, 100, 106, 107

trees..........14, 33, 44, 46, 48, 56

trial 26

tribal 18, 35

tribulation...............................26

tribulations 80

trustworthy 103

U

underappreciated...................80

universe 13, 106

unlawful 28, 29

unveiling 92

utopia...................................108

V

vegetation...................44, 45, 46

veil..69

vice...................................37, 61

vicegerent.............32, 34, 40, 76

vigilance................................20

vineyards 44

virtue 24, 26, 36, 70, 77, 82

virtues 25, 36, 40, 101

virtuous ..20, 21, 68, 77, 94, 102

vision 73, 74, 92, 94

visitation 35

vulnerable 30

W

walk 55, 103

war 35

water...29, 32, 43, 45, 58, 59, 95

wicked 10, 34, 77, 82, 92

wickedness 18, 22

widows 102

wine 58, 59, 61, 62, 63

winter 14

womb 44, 105

woolen 65

Y

yearn 13, 80, 83

youthful 8, 71

Made in the USA
Lexington, KY
28 May 2018